MS-DOS® 5
Quick Reference

Timothy S. Stanley

Library of Congress Catalog Number: 89-60530

ISBN 0-88022-646-3

94   93   92   91   4

Interpretation of the printing code: the rightmost double-digit number is the year of the book's printing; the rightmost single-digit number is the number of the book's printing. For example, a printing code of 90-4 shows that the fourth printing of the book occurred in 1990.

This book is based on MS-DOS Version 5.0.

Que Quick Reference Series

The *Que Quick Reference Series* is a portable resource of essential microcomputer knowledge. Whether you are a new or experienced user, you can rely on the high-quality information contained in these convenient guides.

Drawing on the experience of many of Que's best-selling authors, the *Que Quick Reference Series* helps you easily access important program information.

The *Que Quick Reference Series* includes these titles:

1-2-3 Quick Reference
1-2-3 Release 2.2 Quick Reference
1-2-3 Release 3 Quick Reference
1-2-3 Release 3.1 Quick Reference
Allways Quick Reference
Assembly Language Quick Reference
AutoCAD Quick Reference, 2nd Edition
C Quick Reference
CorelDRAW Quick Reference
dBASE IV Quick Reference
DOS and BIOS Functions Quick Reference
Excel Quick Reference
Hard Disk Quick Reference
Harvard Graphics Quick Reference
MS-DOS 5 Quick Reference
Microsoft Word 5.5 Quick Reference
Norton Utilities Quick Reference
PC Tools Quick Reference, 2nd Edition
Q&A Quick Reference
Quattro Pro Quick Reference
QuickBASIC Quick Reference
Turbo Pascal Quick Reference
UNIX Programmer's Quick Reference
UNIX Shell Commands Quick Reference
Windows 3 Quick Reference
WordPerfect Quick Reference
WordPerfect 5.1 Quick Reference

Publisher
> Lloyd J. Short

Series Product Director
> Karen A. Bluestein

Production Editor
> Cheryl S. Robinson

Editor
> Julie McLaughlin Foster

Technical Editor
> David Knispel

Production Team
> Claudia Bell
> Jill Bomaster
> Betty Kish
> Bob LaRoche
> Kimberly Leslie
> Howard Peirce

Trademark Acknowledgments

1-2-3, Lotus, Symphony, and VisiCalc are registered trademarks of Lotus Development Corporation.

COMPAQ 386 is a trademark, and COMPAQ is a registered trademark of COMPAQ Computer Corporation.

FastBack is a registered trademark of Fifth Generation Systems, Inc.

Hercules Graphics Card is a trademark of Hercules Computer Technology.

IBM and IBM AT are registered trademarks of International Business Machines Corporation.

MS-DOS is a registered trademark of Microsoft Computer, Inc.

PostScript is a registered trademark of Adobe Systems, Inc.

ProKey is a trademark of RoseSoft, Inc.

Quattro Pro and Paradox are registered trademarks and Reflex is a trademark of Borland International, Inc.

SideKick is a registered trademark of Borland International, Inc.

Table of Contents

Introduction

MS-DOS 5 Quick Reference is not a rehash of traditional
documentation. Instead, this quick reference is a
compilation of the most frequently used information
from Que's best-selling DOS books.

MS-DOS 5 Quick Reference gives you essential
information on MS-DOS commands, batch files, the
DOS Editor, and error messages. You learn the proper
use of primary DOS functions, as well as how to avoid
serious errors. Thanks to the MS-DOS Survival Guide,
you also learn the proper DOS commands to use for
specific operations. In all, *MS-DOS 5 Quick Reference*
contains fundamental DOS information in a compact,
easy-to-use format.

Although *MS-DOS 5 Quick Reference* contains essential
DOS information, it is not intended as a replacement for
the comprehensive information presented in a full-size
guide. You should supplement this quick reference with
one of Que's complete MS-DOS texts, such as
*Upgrading To MS-DOS 5, Using MS-DOS 5,
TurboCharging MS-DOS, MS-DOS 5 QuickStart, or
Que's MS-DOS Users Guide Special Edition.*

Now you can put essential information at your fingertips
with *MS-DOS 5 Quick Reference*—and the entire *Que
Quick Reference Series*!

HINTS FOR USING THIS BOOK

The *MS-DOS Quick Reference* includes an alphabetical listing of all MS-DOS commands. Each command is presented in the same format. The command name appears first, followed by the terms *Internal* or *External*. These terms indicate whether the command is built into MS-DOS (internal) or is disk-resident (external).

The command's purpose is explained, followed by the syntax required to invoke the command and the rules for its use. Examples are provided for some of the commands.

The "Notes" section contains additional comments, information, hints, or suggestions for using the command.

Also contained in this book are sections on batch files, the new DOS EDIT feature, DOS messages, and a DOS survival guide.

Conventions

The conventions used in this book have been established to help you learn quickly. Keep these guidelines in mind as you read this book.

File Specifications

A file specification is represented as

   *d:path*filename.*ext*

d: is the name of the disk drive holding the file, and *path* is the directory path to the file. filename is the root name of the file, and *.ext* is the file name extension.

If a notation appears in boldfaced blue uppercase letters, that notation is mandatory and must be entered. If a notation appears in italicized type, the notation is optional and is entered only when appropriate. Words that appear in lowercase letters are variables. Make sure that you substitute the appropriate disk drive letter or name, path name, file name, and so on for the lowercase variable notation.

Commands, as well as all parameters and switches typed with commands, can be typed in either upper- or lowercase letters. The FIND command and the batch subcommands are exceptions to this rule because the case of the letters may be important.

Note that you must follow the file specification. You cannot use notation that does not appear in the file specification syntax. For example, the notation **d:filename.ext** indicates that path names are not allowed in the command.

In most cases, you can substitute a device name for a full file specification.

On-screen messages appear in a `special` typeface.

External Commands and Batch Files

External commands and batch files that reside in different subdirectories can be executed just as program and batch files on different disks. The syntax used in this summary has a *c* added to the disk drive name and path. The notation is

   *dc:pathc***command_name**

dc: is the name of the disk drive that holds the command, *pathc* is the directory path to the command, and **command_name** is the name of the program or batch file.

This notation is valid for batch files and external commands, which are disk-resident commands that are not an internal part of COMMAND.COM.

The following rules apply for external commands and batch files:

- If you do not specify a disk drive name for the command (*dc:*), MS-DOS searches for the command on the current disk drive.

- If you do not specify a path (*pathc*), MS-DOS searches for the command on the current directory of the current disk (or the current directory of the specified disk drive).

- If you do not specify a drive name and a path name, MS-DOS searches the current directory of the current disk for the command. If the command is not found, MS-DOS searches the list of paths specified by the PATH command. If it cannot find the command after searching the path, the error message

```
Bad command or file name
```

is displayed and the MS-DOS system prompt (usually A> or C>) appears.

MS-DOS 5 COMMAND REFERENCE

APPEND

(Set directory search order)   *External*

Purpose

Instructs MS-DOS to search specified directories on specified disks if a nonprogram/nonbatch file is not found in the current directory.

Syntax

To attach APPEND for the first time to the DOS environment and enable APPEND to search the path for data files, use the following syntax:

    *dc:pathc***APPEND** */E* */X:ON*

To attach APPEND for the first time to the DOS environment and enable APPEND to search only the current directory for data files, use the following syntax:

    *dc:pathc***APPEND** */E* */X:OFF*

To establish or change the data file search path, use the following syntax:

    *dc:pathc***APPEND**
    d1:path1;d2:path2;d3:path3;. . .

To temporarily disable searching the path for data files, use the following syntax

    *dc:pathc***APPEND** */PATH:OFF*

To see the search path, use the following syntax:

    dc:pathc**APPEND**

To disconnect the data file search, use the following syntax:

    *dc:pathc***APPEND;**

In the preceding syntax lines, *dc:* is the name of the disk drive holding the command; *pathc* is the path to the command; *d1:*, *d2:*, and *d3:* are valid disk drive names; and *path1*, *path2*, and *path3* are valid path names to the directories in which you want MS-DOS to search for nonprogram/nonbatch files.

Switches

/X:ON|OFF	Searches the path for data files when turned ON. When OFF, searches only the current directory for data files.

/E	Places the disk drive paths in the APPEND environment variable.
/PATH:ON|OFF	Searches the path for data files when turned ON. When OFF, searches only the current directory for data files.

ASSIGN

(Assign disk drive)   ***External***

Purpose

Instructs MS-DOS to use a disk drive other than the one specified by a program or command.

Syntax

To reroute drive activity, use the following syntax:

> *dc:pathc*ASSIGN d1=d2 . . .

dc: is the name of the disk drive holding the command.

pathc is the path to the command.

d1 is the disk drive that the program or MS-DOS normally uses.

d2 is the disk drive that you want the program or DOS to use, instead of the usual drive.

The three periods (. . .) represent additional disk drive assignments.

To view the current assignments, use the following syntax:

> *dc:pathc*ASSIGN /STATUS

To clear the reassignment, use the following syntax:

> *dc:pathc*ASSIGN

Examples

    ASSIGN A = C or ASSIGN A =C

MS-DOS reroutes to drive C any activity for drive A.
A space can appear on either side of the equal sign.

    ASSIGN A=C B=C

MS-DOS reroutes to drive C any requests for activity for
drives A and B.

    ASSIGN /STATUS

MS-DOS displays all drive assignments made.

    ASSIGN

Any previous drive reassignment is cleared.

Note that to ensure compatibility with future versions of
MS-DOS, you should use the SUBST command rather
than ASSIGN.

ATTRIB

(Change/show file attributes)   *External*

Purpose

Displays, sets, or clears a file's read-only, archive,
system, or hidden attributes.

Syntax

To set the file's attributes, use the following syntax:

    *dc:pathc*ATTRIB +R +A +S +H
    *d:path*filename.ext /S

To clear the file's attributes, use the following syntax:

    *dc:pathc*ATTRIB -R -A -S -H
    *d:path*filename.ext /S

To display a file's attribute status, use the following syntax:

*dc:pathc***ATTRIB** *d:path***filename.ext** */S*

dc: is the name of the disk drive holding the command.

pathc is the path to the command.

R is the read-only attribute.

A is the archive attribute.

S is the system file attribute.

H is the hidden attribute.

The + turns on the attribute so that the file becomes read-only, marked as created or changed, marked as a system file, or hidden.

The - turns off the attribute so that you can write to the file, mark the file as not created or changed, mark the file as no longer being a system file, or remove the hidden attribute.

d: is the name of the disk drive that holds the files for which the attribute will be displayed or changed.

path is the path to the files for which the attribute will be displayed or changed.

filename.ext is the name of the file for which the attribute will be displayed or changed. Wildcards are permitted.

Switch

/S	Sets or clears the attributes of the specified files in the current directory and all subsequent directories.

BACKUP

(Back up diskettes or hard disks)   *External*

Purpose

Backs up one or more files from a hard disk or a diskette onto a diskette or another hard disk.

Syntax

> *dc:pathc***BACKUP** **d1:***path\\filename.ext* **d2:**
> */S /M /A /D:date /T:time /F:size*
> */L:d1:path\\filenamel.ext*

dc: is the name of the disk drive that holds the command.

pathc is the path to the command.

d1: is the name of the hard disk or floppy disk drive you want to back up.

path is the initial directory path for backup.

filename.ext is the name of the file(s) you want to back up. Wildcards are allowed.

d2: is the hard disk or floppy disk drive that will receive the backup files.

Examples

To back up the entire hard disk, type

> **BACKUP C:\\ A: /S**

To back up a single directory, type

> **BACKUP C:\\DATA A:**

To back up a single file, type

> **BACKUP C:*.LET A:**

To back up all files that were changed on or after Aug. 21, 1990, type

> **BACKUP C:\\ A: /S /D:8/21/90**

To back up all files in and below the \DATA directory
that changed since the last backup procedure and append
them to the end of the backup disks, type

BACKUP C:\DATA A: /S /M /A

BREAK

(Ctrl-Break Checking) *Internal*

Purpose

Determines when MS-DOS looks for a Ctrl-Break or
Ctrl-C to stop a program.

Syntax

To turn on BREAK, type

BREAK ON

To turn off BREAK, type

BREAK OFF

To find out whether BREAK is on or off, type

BREAK

This command checks during keyboard reads, screen
writes, printer writes, and disk activity.

CHCP

(Change code page) *Internal*

Purpose

Changes the code page (font) used by MS-DOS for all
devices that display fonts.

Syntax

To change the current code page, type

CHCP codepage

To display the current code page, type

CHCP

codepage is a valid three-digit code page number.

CHDIR/CD

(Change directory)   *Internal*

Purpose

Changes the current directory or shows the path of the current directory.

Syntax

To change the current directory, use the following syntax:

CHDIR *d:*path

or

CD *d:*path

To show the current directory path on a disk drive, use the following syntax:

CHDIR *d:*

or

CD *d:*

d: is a valid disk drive name.

path is a valid directory path.

Rules

The following rules apply to the CHDIR/CD command:

- If you do not indicate a disk drive, the current disk drive is used.

- When you specify a path name, MS-DOS moves from the current directory to the last directory specified in the **path**.

- If you want to start the move with the disk's root directory, use the backslash (\) as the path's first character. Otherwise, MS-DOS assumes that the path starts with the current directory.

- If you specify an invalid path, MS-DOS displays an error message and remains in the current directory.

Examples

To direct MS-DOS to move from the root directory to the directory named DOS, type

CD DOS

To direct MS-DOS to move from the root directory to HARDDISK, type

CD DOS\HARDDISK

To direct MS-DOS to move from the \DOS\HARDDISK directory to the DOS directory, type

CHDIR ..

or

CHDIR \DOS

or

CD . .

or

CD\DOS

MS-DOS moves from HARDDISK back to the DOS directory because the double periods represent the parent directory. DOS is the parent directory of HARDDISK. HARDDISK is the child directory of DOS.

CHKDSK

(Check disk)   ***External***

Purpose

Checks the directory and the file allocation table (FAT) of the disk and reports disk and memory status. CHKDSK also can repair errors in the directories or the FAT.

Syntax

*dc:pathc***CHKDSK** *d:path\filename.ext /F/V*

dc: is the name of the disk drive that holds the command.

pathc is the path to the command.

d: is the name of the disk drive you want analyzed.

path is the directory path to the files you want analyzed.

filename.ext is a valid MS-DOS file name. Wildcards are permitted.

Switches

/F   Fixes the file allocation table and other problems when errors are found.

/V   Shows CHKDSK's progress and displays more detailed information about the errors the program finds. (This switch is known as the verbose switch.)

Examples

To instruct MS-DOS to analyze the disk or diskette in the current drive, type

CHKDSK

To instruct MS-DOS to analyze the diskette in drive B, type

CHKDSK B:

To instruct MS-DOS to analyze the diskette in drive A and ask permission to repair the file allocation table (FAT) if a flaw is found, type

CHKDSK A: /F

In case a flaw is encountered, one message may be

```
xxxx lost clusters found in xxx chains

Convert lost chains to files (Y/N)?_
```

If you press Y, CHKDSK converts the lost areas of the disk into files. These files will appear in the root directory of the disk and use the name FILExxxx.CHK, in which xxxx is a consecutive number between 0000 and 9999. If these files do not contain useful information, you can delete them.

To instruct MS-DOS to invoke the verbose mode, which lists each directory and subdirectory on the disk and all files in the directories, type

CHKDSK /V

Note that this output can be redirected to a file or printer.

To instruct MS-DOS to check whether all files in the current directory on the current drive are stored contiguously on the disk, type

CHKDSK *.*

The following messages may be displayed:

```
All specified file(s) are contiguous
```

This message tells you that you are getting good disk performance.

```
d:path\filename.ext
Contains xxx noncontiguous blocks
```

When this message appears, the specified files are not stored contiguously on the disk. The message appears for each file not stored contiguously. If you are analyzing a diskette and many file names are listed, you should COPY (not DISKCOPY) the files to another

diskette. In the case of the hard disk, BACKUP your
entire hard disk, reformat it, and then RESTORE the
files.

CLS

(Clear screen)   *Internal*

Purpose

Erases the display screen.

Syntax

    CLS

Rules

The following rules apply to the CLS command:

- All on-screen information is cleared, and the cursor is
  placed at the home position (upper left corner).

- This command affects only the active video display.

- If you use the ANSI control codes to set the
  foreground and background color settings, the
  settings remain in effect. If you do not set the
  foreground and background colors, the screen reverts
  to light characters on a dark background.

- CLS only affects the screen, not memory.

COMMAND

*(Invoke secondary command
processor)*   *External*

Purpose

Invokes another copy of COMMAND.COM, the
command processor.

Syntax

> *dc:pathc***COMMAND** *comspec cttydevice*
> */E:size /P /C string /MSG*

dc: is the name of the drive where MS-DOS can find a copy of COMMAND.COM.

pathc is the MS-DOS path to the copy of COMMAND.COM.

comspec is the path where COMMAND.COM is located. Sets the COMSPEC environment parameter.

cttydevice is the device used for input and output. The default is CON (the keyboard and screen).

string is the set of characters, such as a command, you pass to the new copy of the command interpreter.

Switches

/E:size	Sets the *size* of the *environment.* Size is a decimal number from 160 to 32,768 bytes, rounded up to the nearest multiple of 16.
/P	Keeps this copy permanently in memory (until the next system reset).
/C	Passes the string of commands (the string) to the new copy of COMMAND.COM.
/MSG	Loads all error messages into memory. You must use this switch with /P.

COMP

(Compare files)   ***External***

Purpose

Compares two sets of disk files to see whether they are the same or different.

Syntax

*dc:pathc***COMP** *d1:path1\\filename1.ext1
d2:path2\\filename2.ext2 /D /A /L /N:lines /C*

dc: is the name of the disk drive holding the command.

pathc is the path to the command.

d1: is the drive containing the first set of files to be compared.

path1 is the path to the first set of files.

filename1.ext1 is the file name for the first set of files. Wildcards are allowed.

d2: is the drive containing the second set of files to be compared.

path2 is the path to the second set of files.

filename2.ext2 is the file name for the second set of files. Wildcards are allowed.

d1 and *d2* may be the same.

path1 and *path2* may be the same.

filename1.ext1 and *filename2.ext2* also may be the same.

Terms

d1:path1\\filename1.ext1 is the primary file set.

d2:path2\\filename2.ext2 is the secondary file set.

Switches

/D	Displays the hexadecimal values of the differing characters.

/A	Displays the actual differing characters.
/L	Displays the line number of the differing characters.
/N:LINE	Compares the number of lines in a file. *line* is the number of lines to compare.
/C	Compares the files regardless of case.

Rules

The following rules apply to the COMP command:

- If you do not specify a drive name or path name for a set, DOS uses the current disk drive and directory. (This rule applies to *d1:path1* and *d2:path2*, as well as to *dc:pathc*, the drive holding the command itself.)

- If you do not enter a file name for a file set, all files for that set (primary or secondary) are compared (which is the same as entering *.*). However, only the files in the secondary set with names matching file names in the primary set are compared.

- If you do not enter a drive name, path name, and file name, COMP prompts you for the primary and secondary file sets and switches to compare. Otherwise, the correct diskettes must be in the correct drive if you are comparing files on diskettes. COMP does not wait for you to insert diskettes if you give both primary and secondary file names.

- Files with matching names but different lengths are not checked. A message is printed indicating that these files are different.

- After ten mismatches (unequal comparisons) between the contents of two compared files, COMP automatically ends the comparison between the two files and aborts.

Notes

If you have a program that once functioned properly, but now acts strangely, check a good backup copy of the file against the copy you are using. If COMP finds differences, copy the good program to the disk you are using.

If you are comparing ASCII files, you may find the /A and /C switches useful. These switches display the actual character differences and do not compare character case. If you are comparing binary files, you may prefer the /D switch to display differences using hexadecimal values rather than decimal values.

To find the last revision of a file, look at its date and time stamp in the directory to identify the most recent revision. If you want to compare diskettes that have been copied with DISKCOPY, use DISKCOMP instead of COMP.

Configuration Subcommand

BREAK (Ctrl-Break Checking)   *Internal*

Purpose

Determines when MS-DOS looks for a Ctrl-Break or Ctrl-C to stop a program.

Syntax

To turn on BREAK, use the following syntax:

BREAK = ON

To turn off BREAK, use the following syntax:

BREAK = OFF

Configuration Subcommand

BUFFERS (Set number of disk buffers) Internal

Purpose

Sets the number of disk buffers set aside by MS-DOS in memory.

Syntax

BUFFERS = nn,*c*

nn is the number of buffers to set, in the range of 1 to 99.

c is the number of sectors, from 1 to 8, that can be read or written at a time. The default is one.

Configuration Subcommand

COUNTRY (Set country-
dependent information)   *Internal*

Purpose

Instructs MS-DOS to modify the input and display of date, time, and field divider information.

Syntax

COUNTRY = nnn,*mmm,d:path\filenamef.extf*

nnn is the country code.

mmm is the code page.

d:path are the drive and directory that contain *filenamef.extf*

filenamef.extf is the file that contains the country information (COUNTRY.SYS).

Configuration Subcommand

DEVICE (Set device driver)   *Internal*

Purpose

Instructs MS-DOS to load, link, and use a special device driver.

Syntax

DEVICE = *d:path*\filename.ext

d: is the name of the drive on which MS-DOS can find the device drive.

path\ is the MS-DOS path to the device driver.

filename.ext is the root file name and optional extension of the device driver.

Configuration Subcommand

DEVICEHIGH (Load device driver in reserved memory)   *Internal*

Purpose

Instructs MS-DOS to load, link, and use a special device driver in the reserved memory of an 80386 or 80486 computer.

Syntax

DEVICEHIGH *SIZE* = *hexbyte*
dd:pathd*filenamed.extd*

SIZE = *hexbyte* is the least amount of reserved memory that must be available for the device driver to be loaded into memory. *hexbyte* is the actual size in bytes expressed as a hexadecimal value.

dd:pathd\ is the disk drive and path on which the device driver is located.

filenamed.extd is the actual file name and extension of the device driver.

Configuration Subcommand

DOS (Load DOS in high memory)   *Internal*

Purpose

Loads DOS into the high memory area of the computer or controls a link between conventional memory and reserved memory. This command requires an 80286 computer or greater with extended memory.

Syntax

To load DOS into high memory, type

DOS = HIGH

To load DOS in high memory and activate upper memory blocks on a 80386 or 80486 computer, type

DOS = HIGH, UMB

Options are as follows:

DOS = *HIGH | LOW, UMB | NOUMB*

HIGH places a portion of DOS into the high memory area.

LOW is the default setting, and causes DOS to reside entirely in conventional memory.

UMB establishes and maintains a link between conventional memory and the upper memory blocks in reserved memory for 80386 and 80486 computers.

NOUMB is the default setting, which disconnects a link between conventional memory and the upper memory blocks in reserved memory for 80386 and 80486 computers.

Configuration Subcommand

DRIVPARM (Define block device)   *Internal*

Purpose

Defines or changes the parameters of a block device, such as a disk drive.

Syntax

DRIVPARM = /D:num /C /F:type /H:hds /I /N /S:sec /T:trk

Switches

/D:num	Specifies the drive number, **num**, ranging from 0 to 255, where drive A=0, drive B=1, drive C=2, and so on.
/C	Specifies that the drive supports *change-line*, meaning that the drive has sensor support to determine when the drive door is open. When the drive door is open, the drive is sensed as empty.
/F:type	Determines the type of drive. *type* is one of the following:

type	Drive specification
0	160K/320K/180K/360K
1	1.2M
2	720K

3	Single-density 8" disk
4	Double-density 8" disk
5	Hard disk
6	Tape drive
7	1.44M

Type 2 is the default if you do not specify /F.

/H:hds	Specifies the total number of drive heads, where *hds* is a number from 1 to 99. The default for *hds* is 2.
/I	Use if you have a 3 1/2-inch drive connected internally to your floppy drive controller, but your ROM BIOS does not support a 3 1/2-inch drive.
/N	Specifies that your drive or other block device is not removable, or a hard disk, for example.
/S:sec	Specifies the total number of sectors per side on the drive. *sec* can be a number from 1 to 999.
/T:trk	Specifies the number of tracks per side of a disk or the total number of tracks per tape. *trk* can be a number from 1 to 99.

Configuration Subcommand

FCBS (set control blocks)   *Internal*

Purpose

Specifies the number of MS-DOS File Control Blocks
that can be open concurrently.

Syntax

    FCBS = maxopen

maxopen is the number of FCBs that can be open at any
given time.

Configuration Subcommand

FILES (set maximum open files)   *Internal*

Purpose

Specifies the number of file handles that may be open at
any given time.

Syntax

    FILES = nnn

nnn is the number of file handles that may be open at
any given time.

Configuration Subcommand

INSTALL (Load TSR in memory)   *Internal*

Purpose

Starts a program from CONFIG.SYS. Valid programs
to start with INSTALL are FASTOPEN, KEYB,
NLSFUNC, SHARE, and other programs that remain in
the computer's random-access memory (TSR).

Syntax

INSTALL = *dc:pathc***filename.ext** *options*

dc:pathc are the disk drive and the directory that hold the command.

filename.ext is the name of the file, which may be FASTOPEN.EXE, KEYB.EXE, NLSFUNC.EXE, SHARE.EXE, or other valid terminate and stay resident programs.

options are any parameters the **filename.ext** command requires.

Configuration Subcommand

LASTDRIVE (specify last system drive)   *Internal*

Purpose

Sets the last valid drive letter acceptable to MS-DOS.

Syntax

LASTDRIVE = x

x is the alphabetical character for the highest system drive. You can use single letters from A to Z.

Configuration Subcommand

REM (Remark)   *Internal*

Purpose

Places remarks or hidden statements in the CONFIG.SYS file.

Syntax

REM *remark*

remark is any text that you want to insert into the CONFIG.SYS file.

Configuration Subcommand

SHELL (specify command processor)   Internal

Purpose

Changes the default MS-DOS command processor.

Syntax

SHELL = *d:path***filename.ext**

d: is the name of the drive where MS-DOS can find the command processor.

path is the MS-DOS path to the command processor.

filename.ext is the root file name and optional extension of the command processor.

Configuration Subcommand

STACKS (Allocate interrupt storage)   Internal

Purpose

Allots memory storage when a hardware interrupt occurs.

Syntax

STACKS = n,*m*

n is the number of allotted stacks. The default for computers using the 8088/8086 microprocessor is 0, whereas the default for those computers using the 80286, 80386sx, and 80386 is 9.

m is the size in bytes of each stack. The default for computers using the 8088/8086 microprocessor is 0, whereas the default for those computers using the 80286, 80386sx, and 80386 is 128.

COPY

(Copy files)   *Internal*

Purpose

Copies files between disk drives or devices, either keeping the same file name or changing it. COPY can concatenate (join) two or more files into another file or append one or more files to another file. Options support special handling of text files and verification of the copying process.

Syntax

To copy a file, use the following syntax:

> COPY */A/B d1:path1\filename1.ext1/A/B*
> *d0:path2/filename0.ext0 /A/B/V*

or

> COPY */A/B d1:path1\filename1.ext1/A/B/V*

To join several files into one file, use the following:

> COPY */A/B d1:path1\filename1.ext1/A/B*
> *+ d2:path2\filename2.ext2/A/B +. . .*

d1:, d2:, and *d0:* are valid disk drive names.

path1\, path2\, and path0 are valid path names.

filename1.*ext1*, filename2.*ext2*, and filename0.*ext0* are valid file names. Wildcards are allowed.

The three periods (. . .) represent additional files in the form *dx:pathx/filenamex.extx.*

Terms

The file from which you are copying is the *source file*. The names containing **1** and **2** are the source files.

The file to which you are copying is the *destination file*. It is represented by a **0**.

Switches

/V   Verifies that the copy has been recorded correctly.

The following switches have different effects for the source file and the destination file.

For the source file

/A   Treats the file as an ASCII (text) file. The command copies all the information in the file up to, but not including, the end-of-file marker (Ctrl-Z). Anything after the end-of-file marker is ignored.

/B   Copies the entire file as if it were a program file (*binary1*). Any end-of-file markers (Ctrl-Z) are treated as normal characters, and the EOF characters are copied.

For the destination file

/A   Adds an end-of-file marker (Ctrl-Z) to the end of the ASCII text file after it is copied.

/B   Does not add the end-of-file marker to this binary file.

CTTY

(Change console)   *Internal*

Purpose

Changes the standard input and output device to an auxiliary console, or changes the input and output device back from an auxiliary console to the keyboard and video display.

Syntax

CTTY device

device is the name of the device you want to use as the new standard input and output device. This name must be a valid MS-DOS device name.

Rules

The following rules apply to CTTY:

- The **device** should be a character-oriented device capable of both input and output.

- Programs designed to work with the video display's control codes may not function properly when redirected.

Examples

To make the device attached to COM1 the new console, type

CTTY COM1

The peripheral connected to COM1 must be a terminal or a teleprinter (printer with a keyboard). After you issue this command, MS-DOS expects normal input to come from COM1 and sends anything for the video display to COM1.

To make the keyboard and video display the console, thus cancelling the previous CTTY, type

CTTY CON:

Notes

With the CTTY command, a terminal or teleprinter, instead of the computer's keyboard and video display, can be used for console input and output. This added versatility has little effect on most users.

You must specify a device that can receive input and send output to the computer system. Using CTTY with a normal printer (an output-only device) is a mistake because MS-DOS waits forever for you to type commands on the printer's nonexistent keyboard.

═**DATE** ╞═══════════════════════════

(Set/show date)   *Internal*

Purpose

Displays and/or changes the system date.

Syntax

DATE *date_string*

date_string is in one of the following forms:

- *mm-dd-yy* or *mm-dd-yyyy* for North America
- *dd-mm-yy* or *dd-mm-yyyy* for Europe
- yy-mm-dd or yyyy-mm-dd for the Far East

mm is a one- or two-digit number for the month (1 to 12).

dd is a one- or two-digit number for the day (1 to 31).

yy is a one- or two-digit number for the year (80 to 99). The 19 is assumed.

yyyy is a four-digit number for the year (1980 to 2099).

Note

You can use hyphens, periods, or slashes as the delimiters between the day, month, and year. The result displayed varies, depending on the country code set in the CONFIG.SYS file.

═**DEBUG** ╞═══════════════════════════

V1, V2, V3, V4, V5   *External*

Purpose

Enables you to test and edit programs.

Syntax

*dc:path*c**DEBUG** *de:path*e*filename.ext*e

dc:pathc are the disk drive and directory that hold the command.

de:pathe are the disk drive and directory that hold the file you want to edit.

filename.exte is the file you want to load into memory and edit.

⧣DEL

(Delete files)   *Internal*

Purpose

Deletes files from the disk.

DEL is an alternative command for ERASE and performs the same functions. See *ERASE* for a complete description.

⧣DELOLDOS

V5   *External*

Purpose

Removes all pre-DOS 5 DOS files from the hard disk.

Syntax

   *dc:pathc***DELOLDOS /B**

dc:pathc are the disk drive and directory that hold the command.

Switch

   /B   Starts DELOLDOS in Black and White mode.

Note

When you upgrade an existing DOS system to DOS 5, the old version of DOS is preserved. Use this command to delete entirely the old version of DOS.

DIR

(Directory)   *Internal*

Purpose

Lists any or all files and subdirectories in a disk's directory.

The DIR command displays the following information:

- Disk volume name (if any)
- Disk volume serial number
- Name of the directory (its complete path)
- Name of each disk file or subdirectory
- Number of files
- Amount, in bytes, of displayed files
- Amount, in bytes, of free space on the disk
- Unless otherwise directed, also shows the number of bytes occupied by each file and the date/time of the file's creation/last update

Syntax

DIR *d:path\filename.ext* /P/W /A:attr /O:order /S /B /L

d: is the drive holding the disk you want to examine.

path is the path to the directory you want to examine.

filename.ext is a valid file name. Wildcards are permitted.

Switches

/P	Pauses when the screen is full and waits for you to press any key.
/W	Gives a wide (80-column) display of the names of the files. The information about file size, date, and time is not displayed.

/A:attrib — Displays only those files that have the attribute that you specify. The settings for *attrib* are given in the following table.

attrib	Description
(/A only)	Displays all directory entries, even system and hidden files.
h	Displays hidden files.
-h	Displays files that are not hidden.
s	Displays system files.
-s	Displays files that are not system files.
d	Displays subdirectories.
-d	Displays only files (no subdirectory names).
a	Displays files for archiving.
-a	Displays files that have been archived.
r	Displays read-only files.
-r	Displays files that can be read and written to.

/O:sort — Displays the directory in sorted order. The settings for *sort* are given in the following table:

(/O only)	Sorts directory entries alphabetically, listing subdirectories before files (0-9, A-Z).

n		Sorts alphabetically by root name (0-9, A-Z).
-n		Sorts reverse-alphabetically by root name (Z-A, 9-0).
e		Sorts alphabetically by extension (0-9, A-Z).
-e		Sorts reverse-alphabetically by extension (Z-A, 9-0).
d		Sorts by date and time, earliest to latest.
-d		Sorts by date and time, latest to earliest.
s		Sorts by size, smallest to largest.
-s		Sorts by size, largest to smallest.
g		Lists subdirectories before files.
-g		Lists subdirectories after files.
/S		Lists all files in the current directory and all subsequent directories.
/B		Lists root name and extension with period; FILENAME.EXT. No other information such as size, date, and time created are listed.
/L		Lists file names and subdirectory names in lowercase.

Notes

The DIR command finds the disk files or subdirectories on the disk. Unless you use the /S switch, this command shows only the files and subdirectories in the specified or the default directory.

Using the /A switch, you may list only those files with
certain attributes. Listing files that can be archived
enables you to determine which archived files you may
back up or XCOPY. You also may sort files in many
different ways, which enables you to better manage your
files.

DISKCOMP

(Compare diskettes)   *External*

Purpose

Compares two diskettes on a track-for-track, sector-for-
sector basis to see whether their contents are identical.

Syntax

*dc:pathc***DISKCOMP** *d1: d2: /1 /8*

dc: is the name of the disk drive holding the command.

pathc is the path to the command.

d1: and *d2:* are the disk drives that hold the diskettes
you want to compare. These drives may be the same or
different.

Switches

/1   Compares only the first side of the diskette, even
      if the diskette or disk drive is double-sided.

/8   Compares only eight sectors per track, even if the
      first diskette has a different number of sectors per
      track.

Rules

The following rules apply to DISKCOMP:

- If you do not specify a drive name, the first floppy
  disk drive (usually drive A) is used.

- If you specify only one valid floppy disk drive name,
  it is used for the comparison.

- Giving the same valid floppy disk drive name twice is the same as specifying only one disk drive name.

- If you specify a valid hard disk drive name or invalid disk drive name, MS-DOS displays an error message and does not perform the comparison.

- When you are using one disk drive, MS-DOS prompts you to change diskettes.

- Only compatible diskettes should be compared. The two diskettes must be formatted with the same number of tracks, sectors, and sides.

- Do not use DISKCOMP with an ASSIGNed disk drive. DISKCOMP ignores the effects of the ASSIGN.

- Do not use a JOINed disk, a SUBSTituted disk, a virtual (RAM) disk, or networked disk drives with DISKCOMP. MS-DOS displays an error message.

Example

DISKCOMP A: B:

MS-DOS compares the diskette in drive A with the diskette in drive B.

DISKCOPY

(Copy entire diskette)   *External*

Purpose

Copies the entire contents of one diskette to another diskette on a track-for-track basis (making a "carbon copy"). DISKCOPY works with diskettes only.

Syntax

*dc:pathc***DISKCOPY** *d1: d2: /1/ V*

dc: is the name of the disk drive that holds the command.

pathc is the path to the command.

d1: is the floppy disk drive that holds the source (original) diskette.

d2: is the floppy disk drive that holds the diskette to which you want to copy (target diskette).

Switches

/1   Copies only the first side of the diskette.

/V   Verifies each track after it has been copied.

Terms

The diskette from which you are copying is the *source* or *first* diskette.

The diskette to which you are copying is the *target* or *second* diskette.

DOSKEY

(Review command line/Create macros)   External

Purpose

Remembers a history of commands typed from the command line for reuse or editing. You also can use macros to create custom DOS commands.

Syntax

dc:pathc **DOSKEY** */REINSTALL*
/BUFSIZE=bytes /MACROS /HISTORY
/INSERT or IOVERSTRIKE
macroname=macrotext

dc:pathc is the drive and subdirectory where DOSKEY is located.

macroname is the name assigned to the command or commands you want to perform.

macrotext is the command or commands that are performed when you type the *macroname* and press **Enter**.

Switches

/REINSTALL	Reinstalls DOSKEY.
/BUFSIZE=bytes	Sets aside memory for DOSKEY to store commands and macros. The value of *bytes* is the actual amount of memory to set aside. The default is 1024 bytes, or 1K bytes.
/MACROS	Lists all the macros created with DOSKEY.
/HISTORY	Lists all commands stored in memory from earliest to latest.
/INSERT or /OVERSTRIKE	Enables Insert mode or Overstrike mode. With Insert mode, you can insert characters when editing a command line.

Notes

With DOSKEY, a history of commands is stored in memory. The number of commands retained in memory depends on the buffer size, which is, by default, 1K of memory. When the buffer is full, the oldest command is eliminated, making room for the new command. The buffer also contains macros as well as a history of commands.

To recall a command in the history, use the following keys:

Key	*Function*
Up arrow	Displays the last command in the history.
Down arrow	Displays the next command in the history. When the last command is reached, the first command is displayed again.

| PgUp | Displays the first command in the history. |
| PgDn | Displays the last command in the history. |

You can use several keys and key combinations to edit a command on the command line in addition to the standard DOS editing keys. These keys and key combinations are as follows:

Key(s)	*Function*
Left arrow	Moves the cursor one character to the left.
Ctrl-left arrow	Moves the cursor one word to the left.
Right arrow	Moves the cursor one character to the right.
Ctrl-right arrow	Moves the cursor one word to the right.
Home	Moves the cursor to the first character in the command line.
End	Moves the cursor after the last character in the command line.
Esc	Erases the current command line.
F7	Lists all commands in the history, numbers each command, and indicates the current command.
Alt-F7	Erases all the commands in the history.
F9	Enables you to specify the number of the command in the history you want to make current. You can press F7 to see the command numbers.

| F10 | Lists all macros in memory. |
| Alt-F10 | Erases all macros in memory. |

DOSKEY enables you to create macros similar to a batch file. By typing the name of a macro, and pressing **Enter**, you can perform several commands. Note that when you develop macros, a few characters are created by the following dollar sign equivalents:

Code	*Description*
$g or $G	Redirects output. Same as >.
$l or $L	Redirects input. Same as <.
$b or $B	Pipes the output of one command as the input of a second command. Same as $vb.
$t or $T	Separates macro commands.
$$	Uses the dollar sign in the command line.
$1 through $9	Specifies replaceable parameters. Same as %1 through %9 in a batch file.
$*	Specifies a replaceable parameter that represents everything typed on the command line after the macro name.

When you create a macro, you can include any valid DOS command, including batch files. Although you can start a batch file from a macro, you cannot start a macro from a batch file.

Examples

To start DOSKEY, use this form:

DOSKEY

To create a macro for moving files, use this form:

DOSKEY MOVE=COPY $1 $2 $T DEL $1

To list all macros in memory, use this form:

DOSKEY /MACROS

To use DOSKEY to record batch files, follow these steps:

1. Type the commands you want to record.

2. Type **DOSKEY /HISTORY > 123.BAT** to save the commands to the batch file.

=DOSSHELL

(Start the Shell program)   *External*

Purpose

Starts the Shell that accompanies DOS.

Syntax

To start the DOS Shell in a different screen mode, type

*dc:pathc***DOSSHELL***/T:screen /G:screen /B*

To start the DOS Shell in the default screen mode, type

*dc:pathC***DOSSHELL**

dc:pathc is the disk drive and subdirectory where DOSSHELL is located.

Switches

/T:screen	Displays the DOS Shell in text mode, using the resolution described by screen.
/G:screen	Displays the DOS Shell in graphics mode, using the resolution described by screen.
/B	Starts the DOS Shell in black and white rather than color.

Video Display Modes

Switch	*Monochrome/ CGA Monitor*	*EGA Monitor*	*VGA Monitor*
/T:L	25 lines	25 lines	25 lines
/T:M	x	43 lines	43 lines
/T:M1	x	43 lines	43 lines
/T:M2	x	43 lines	50 lines
/T:H	x	43 lines	43 lines
/t:H1	x	43 lines	43 lines
/T:H2	x	43 lines	50 lines
/G:L	25 lines	25 lines	25 lines
/G:M	x	43 lines	30 lines
/G:M1	x	43 lines	30 lines
/G:M2	x	43 lines	34 lines
/G:H	x	43 lines	43 lines
/G:H1	x	43 lines	43 lines
/G:H2	x	43 lines	60 lines

Note

DOSSHELL is a user interface that can make DOS easier to use.

═EDIT═════════════════════

(Full-screen text editor)   ***External***

Purpose

Enables you to edit text files (such as batch files) in a full-screen mode. This mode gives you much of the editing capability of a simple word processor.

Syntax

> *dc:pathc***EDIT** *d:path\filename.ext /B /G /H /NOHI*

dc:pathc is the disk drive and subdirectory on which DOSSHELL is located.

d:path\filename.ext is the location and the file you want to edit.

Switches

/B	Places EDIT in Black & White screen colors.
/G	Writes quickly to a CGA monitor. This switch may cause "snow" on some monitors.
/H	Displays the maximum lines that your screen supports (43 for EGA and 50 for VGA).
/NOHI	Uses reverse video rather than high-intensity characters (for LCD screens).

Note

EDIT is the text editor that QBasic uses. You will find this program helpful for creating and editing batch files, as well as other text files. Although DOS still contains EDLIN, EDIT is much superior.

EMM386

(EMS/UMB provider)   *External*

Purpose

Emulates expanded memory (EMS 4.0) on an 80386sx, 80386, and 80486 computer. Also enables device drivers and TSRs to be placed in reserved memory.

Syntax

As a device driver, use the following syntax:

> DEVICE = *dc:pathc*\EMM386.EXE *ramval*
> *w=ON|OFF Ms FRAME=xxxx /Pn=xxxx*
> *X=xxxx-xxxx B=xxxx L=xms A=regs H=hhh*
> *RAM|NOEMS*

As a command, use the following syntax:

> *dc:pathc*\EMM386 *ON | OFF |*
> *AUTO W=ON |* OFF */?*

dc:pathc\ is the disk drive and subdirectory on which EMM386 is located.

Device Driver parameters

ramval is the amount of RAM in one-kilobyte sections you want assigned as EMS 4.0 memory. Enter a value from 16 to 32768 as a multiple of 16 (16, 32, 48,..., 32752, 32768). Any number that you enter, however, is rounded to the nearest 16th. The default is 256.

W=ON|OFF enables or disables support for the Weitek Coprocessor. The default is w=OFF.

Ms is used to specify the segment base address. *s* is a number used to represent the address. This number is the beginning address of the EMS page frame. The numbers and associated hexadecimal addresses are as follows:

1	C000
2	C400
3	C800
4	CC00
5	D000
6	D400
7	D800
8	DC00
9	E000
10	8000
11	8400
12	8800
13	8C00
14	9000

FRAME=xxxx specifies the beginning address of the EMS page frame. *xxxx* may be one of the addresses listed under *Ms*.

/Pxxxx specifies the beginning address just as *FRAME=xxxx* does.

Pn=xxxx defines an address for a page segment. *n* is the numbers 0, 1, 2, 3, 254, 255. To remain compatible with EMS 3.2, P0 through P3 must be contiguous addresses. You cannot use this option if you use *Ms*, *FRAME=xxxx* or */Pxxxx*.

X=xxxx-xxxx specifies that a range of memory should not be used for the EMS page frame. *xxxx-xxxx* are the ranges to keep free.

B=xxxx specifies the lowest address to use for bank switching. The default is 4000.

L=xmsmem specifies the number of one-kilobyte sections that will remain as extended memory, rather than being converted to EMS memory. *xmsmem* is the value of 1K bytes of memory. In order for 1M to remain as extended memory, use the options L=1024.

A=regs is used to allocate the number of alternate registers that EMM386 may use. Although the default number is 7, you can specify a number from 0 to 254 for *regs*.

H=hhh enables you to change from the default 64 handles that EMM386 uses. *hhh* may be a number from 2 to 255.

RAM\NOEMS is used to allocate reserved memory, such as placing some extended memory in open areas in the 640K - 1M address space. *RAM* leaves room for an EMS page frame in the reserved area, but *NOEMS* allocates room for the EMS page frame as additional reserved memory.

Command parameters

ON enables expanded memory.

OFF disables expanded memory.

AUTO enables expanded Weitek Coprocessor support when a program requests it.

W=ON | *OFF* enables or disables, respectively, Weitek Coprocessor support.

Notes

EMM386.EXE must be installed as a device driver before you can use EMM386.EXE as a command at the command line. When installed, 256K of extended memory (or the value that you specify) is used as EMS 4.0 expanded memory.

You can place device drivers and TSR programs into reserved memory by using the RAM or NOEMS options of EMM386. Use NOEMS only if you do not want to enable expanded memory, but would rather use the extra reserved memory area.

EMM386, when used from the DOS command line, controls the settings of the counterpart device driver.

To install EMM386 from CONFIG.SYS (assuming that EMM386.EXE is in C:\DOS), allocating 1M or EMS memory and enabling reserved memory, use the form:

DEVICE=C:\DOS\EMM386.EXE 1024 RAM

To install EMM386 from CONFIG.SYS (assuming that EMM386.EXE is in C:\DOS), disabling expanded memory, use the form:

DEVICE=C:\DOS\EMM386.EXE NOEMS

To temporarily disable expanded memory, use the form:

EMM386 OFF

ERASE

(Erase files)   *Internal*

Purpose

Removes one or more files from the directory.

ERASE *d:path\filename.ext /P*

or

DEL *d:path\filename.ext /P*

d: is the name of the disk drive that holds the file or files you want erased.

path is the directory of the file or files you want erased.

filename.ext is the name of the file or files you want erased. Wildcards are permitted.

Switch

/P   Prompts for a response before a file is deleted.

EXE2BIN

(Change .EXE files into .BIN or .COM files)   *External*

Purpose

Changes suitably formatted .EXE files into .BIN or .COM files.

Syntax

*dc:pathc***EXE2BIN** *d1:path1/***filename1***.ext1*
d2:path2/filename2.ext2

dc: is the name of the disk drive that holds the command.

pathc is the path to the command.

d1: is the name of the disk drive that holds the file you want to convert.

path1/ is the directory of the file you want converted.

filename1 is the root name of the file you want converted.

.ext1 is the extension name of the file you want converted.

d2: is the name of the disk drive for the output file.

path2/ is the directory of the output file.

filename2 is the root name of the output file.

.ext2 is the extension name of the output file.

Terms

The file you want to convert is the *source* file.

The output file is the *destination* file.

Rules

The following rules apply to EXE2BIN:

- If you do not specify a drive for the source file, the current drive is used.

- If you do not specify a drive for the destination file, the source drive is used.

- When you do not specify a path, the current directory of the disk is used.

- You must specify a root name for the source file (the file to be converted).

- If you do not specify a root name for the destination file, the root name of the source file is used.

- If you do not specify an extension for the source file, the extension .EXE is used.

- If you do not specify an extension for the destination file, the extension .BIN is used.

- The .EXE file must be in the correct format (following Microsoft conventions).

Notes

EXE2BIN is a programming utility that converts .EXE (executable) program files to .COM or .BIN (binary image) files. The resulting program takes less disk space and loads faster. This conversion, however, may be a disadvantage in future versions of MS-DOS.

EXIT

(Leave secondary command processor)   *Internal*

Purpose

Leaves a secondary command processor and returns to the primary command processor.

Syntax

EXIT

Note

This command has no effect if a secondary command processor is not loaded or if it was loaded with the */P* switch.

FASTOPEN

(Fast opening of files)   *External*

Purpose

Keeps directory information in memory.

Syntax

*dc:pathc***FASTOPEN d:**=*nnn . . . /X*

dc: is the name of the disk drive that holds the command.

pathc is the path to the command.

d: is the name of the disk drive whose directory information should be held in memory.

nnn is the number of directory entries to be held in memory (10 to 999).

. . . designates additional disk drives in the form **d:**=*nnn*.

Switch

/X	Creates the cache in expanded memory (EMS 4.0 only).

FC

(Compare files)   ***External***

Purpose

Compares two sets of disk files.

Syntax

> *dc:pathc*FC */A /C /L /Lb x /N /T /W /xxxx /B*
> *d1:path1\filename1.ext1 d2:path2\filename2.ext2*

dc: is the name of the disk drive that holds the command.

pathc is the path to the command.

d1: is the drive that contains the first set of files to be compared.

path1 is the path to the first set of files.

filename1.ext is the file name for the first set of files. You can use wildcards.

d2: is the drive containing the second set of files to be compared.

path2 is the path to the second set of files.

filename2.ext 2 is the file name for the second set of files. You can use wildcards.

Note: *d1* and *d2* and *path1* and *path2* may be identical. *filename1.ext1* and *filename2.ext2* also may be identical.

Terms

d1:path1\filename1.ext1 is the primary file set.

d2:path2\filename2.ext2 is the secondary file set.

Switches

/A	Abbreviates ASCII comparison displays.
/B	Forces a binary file comparison.

/C	Causes DOS to disregard the case of letters.
/L	Compares files in ASCII mode.
/LB x	Sets internal buffer to x lines. Also sets maximum number of mismatches before exiting.
/N	Displays line numbers for ASCII comparisons.
/T	Suppresses expansion of tabs to spaces.
/W	Compresses tabs and spaces.
/xxxx	Sets the number of lines (1-9) to match. The default is 2.

Rules

The following rules apply to the FC command:

- You must specify both the primary and secondary file specification.

- Only normal disk files are checked. Hidden or system files and directories are not checked.

Note

Although FC has a similar function to COMP, FC is a more intelligent file compare utility because it makes determinations about the files that it compares and assumes that .EXE, .COM, .SYS, .OBJ, .LIB, and .BIN files are binary. Other files are compared as ASCII files.

=FDISK

(Create a hard disk partition)   *External*

Purpose

Partitions a hard disk.

Syntax

> *dc:pathc*FDISK

Note

You must use FORMAT on a newly partitioned drive.

FIND

(Find string filter)   *External*

Purpose

Displays from the designated files all the lines that match (or do not match) the specified string. This command also can display the line numbers.

Syntax

> *dc:pathc*FIND /V/C/N/I *"string"*
> *d:path\filename.ext...*

dc: is the name of the disk drive holding the command.

pathc is the path to the command.

"string" is the set of characters for which you want to search. You must enclose *string* in quotation marks.

d: is the name of the disk drive for the file.

path is the directory holding the file.

filename.ext is the name of the file that you want to search.

Switches

/V   Displays all lines that do not contain *string*.

/C   Counts the number of times that *string* occurs in the file, but does not display the lines.

/N   Displays the line number (number of the line in the file) before each line that contains *string*.

/I   Performs a non-case-sensitive search.

FORMAT

(Format disk)   *External*

Purpose

Initializes a disk to accept MS-DOS information and files. FORMAT also checks the disk for defective tracks and (optionally) places MS-DOS on the diskette or hard disk.

Syntax

*dc:pathc***FORMAT** *d: /Q/U/S/1/8/ B/4/F:size/N:ss/T:tt/V:label*

dc: is the name of the disk drive that holds the command.

pathc is the path to the command.

d: is the valid disk drive name.

Switches

/S	Places a copy of the operating system on the disk so that you can boot it.
/1	Formats only the first side of the floppy disk.
/8	Formats an eight-sector floppy disk (V1 compatible).
/B	Formats any disk and leaves enough room on the disk to copy the operating system files to the disk so that the disk can be bootable.
/4	Formats a floppy disk in a 1.2M disk drive for double-density (320K/360K) use.
/N:ss	Formats the disk with *ss* number of sectors, with *ss* ranging from 1 to 99.
T:ttt	Formats the disk with *ttt* number of tracks per side, with *ttt* ranging from 1 to 999.

/F:size   Formats the disk to less than maximum capacity, with *size* designating one of the following values:

Drive	*Allowable Values for Size*
160K, 180K	160, 160K, 160KB, 180, 180K, 180KB
320K, 360K	All of above, plus 320, 320K, 320KB, 360, 360K, 360KB
1.2M	All of above, plus 1200, 1200K, 1200KB, 1.2, 1.2M, 1.2MB
720K	720, 720K, 720KB
1.44M	All for 720K, plus 1440, 1440K, 1440KB, 1.44, 1.44M, 1.44MB
2.88M	2880, 2880K, 2880KB, 2.88, 2.88M, 2.88MB

/V:label   Transfers volume label to formatted disk. Replaces label with 11-character name for new disk.

/U   Formats a disk unconditionally. Erases any data that existed on the disk and does not have the ability to recover the information.

/Q   Performs a quick format on the disk, erasing only the file allocation table and root directory. Does not recheck the disk for bad sectors.

Rules

The following rules apply to the FORMAT command:

- Unless otherwise directed through a switch, MS-DOS formats the diskette to its maximum capacity.

- Some switches do not work together. For example, you cannot use the following switch combinations:

  /V or /S with /B.
  /V with /8.
  /N or /T with a 320/360K or hard disk drive.
  /1, /4, /8, or /B with a hard disk.
  /Q with /U.

- Format /U destroys any previously recorded information on the disk.

- To use a diskette with all versions of MS-DOS, use the /B and /1 switches. (Format the diskette for any MS-DOS version and format only one side.)

- A volume name can be 1 to 11 characters long and contain any characters that are legal in a file name.

- If you use the /S switch (to place the operating system on a disk) and the current directory does not contain a copy of MS-DOS, you are prompted to insert the MS-DOS diskette into drive A so that the system receives the copy of the operating system before formatting the disk.

- If MS-DOS formats a hard disk that contains a volume label, it asks

  ```
  Enter current Volume Label for drive d:
  ```

  To continue formatting disk drive *d*, enter the disk drive's current volume label. If you do not enter the exact volume label, FORMAT displays

  ```
  Invalid Volume ID

  Format Failure
  ```

  FORMAT then aborts the procedure.

- If you are formatting a hard disk without a volume label, FORMAT displays

  ```
  WARNING, ALL DATA ON NON-REMOVABLE DISK
  DRIVE d: WILL BE LOST!

  Proceed with Format (Y/N?)
  ```

Answer **Y** to format the hard disk drive, **N** to abort the format.

- Although you can use the /4 switch to create double-sided 5 1/4-inch diskettes in a high-capacity 5 1/4-inch disk drive, the formatted diskette is not reliable when you use it in double-sided disk drives.

GRAFTABL

(Load graphics table)   *External*

Purpose

Loads into memory the additional character sets to be displayed on the Color/Graphics Adapter (CGA).

Syntax

To install or change the table used by the CGA, use this command:

    *dc:pathc***GRAFTABL** *codepage*

To display the number of the current table, use this command:

    *dc:pathc***GRAFTABL /STATUS**

dc: is the name of the disk drive that holds the command.

pathc is the path to the command.

codepage is the three-digit number of the code page for the display.

GRAPHICS

(Graphics screen print)   *External*

Purpose

Prints the graphics screen contents on a suitable printer.

> *dc:pathc***GRAPHICS** *printer filename /R /B /LCD /PRINTBOX:x*

dc:pathc are the disk drive and the directory that hold the command.

printer is the type of printer you are using. The printer can be one of the following:

COLOR1

COLOR4

COLOR8

COMPACT

GRAPHICS

THERMAL

GRAPHICSWIDE

HPDEFAULT

DESKJET

LASERJETII

PAINTJET

QUIETJET

QUIETJET PLUS

RUGGED WRITER

RUGGED WRITERWIDE

THINKJET

filename	Name of the file containing printer information. If no file name is specified, DOS uses the name GRAPHICS.PRO.

Switches

/R	Reverses colors so that the image on the paper matches the screen—a white image on black background.
/B	Prints the background in color. You can use this switch only when the printer type is COLOR4 or COLOR8.
/LCD	Prints the image as displayed on the PC Convertible's LCD display.
/PRINTBOX:x	Prints the image and uses the print box size *id* represented by *x*. This value must match the first entry of a Printbox statement in the printer profile, such as *lcd* or *std*.

Rules

The following rules apply to GRAPHICS:

- If you use this command to print the graphics screen contents, your printer must be compatible with one of the listed printers.

- If you do not specify a *printer*, a Graphics Matrix Printer is assumed.

- If you do not use the /R (reverse) switch, an inverse image is printed, black on white. White images on the screen are printed as dark colors, and black images are printed as white.

- If you do not use the /B switch, the background color of the screen is not printed. The /B switch has no effect unless you specify the printer type COLOR4 or COLOR8.

- When you choose the 320-by-200 (medium-resolution) mode, the printer prints in four shades of gray, corresponding to the four possible colors. When you specify the 640-by-200 (high-resolution) mode, the printer prints in black and white, but the printout is rotated 90 degrees to the left. (The upper right corner of the screen is placed on the upper left corner of the printout.)

- The only way to deactivate GRAPHICS is to reset your computer.

JOIN

(Join disk drives) *External*

Purpose

Produces a single directory structure by connecting a disk drive to a subdirectory of a second disk drive.

Syntax

To connect disk drives, use the following syntax:

*dc:pathc***JOIN d1:** *d2:***directoryname**

To disconnect disk drives, use this syntax:

*dc:pathc***JOIN d1:** /D

To show currently connected drives, use this syntax:

*dc:pathc***JOIN**

dc: is the name of the disk drive holding the command.

pathc is the path to the command.

d1: is the name of the disk drive to be connected.

d2: is the name of the disk drive to which **d1:** is connected.

\\directoryname is the name of a subdirectory in the root directory of d2 (the host). **\\directoryname** holds the connection to **d1** (the guest).

Switch

/D   Disconnects the specified guest disk drive from its host.

Terms

The disk drive being connected is called the *guest disk drive*.

The disk drive and the subdirectory to which the guest disk drive is connected are the *host disk drive* and the *host subdirectory*.

KEYB

(Enable foreign language keys)   **External**

Purpose

Changes the keyboard layout and characters to one of five non-English languages.

Syntax

To change the current keyboard layout, use this syntax:

> *dc:pathc***KEYB** *keycode, codepage,*
>   *d:path***KEYBOARD.SYS** */ID:code /E*

To display the current values for KEYB, use this syntax:

> *dc:pathc:***KEYB**

dc:pathc are the disk drive and the directory that hold the command.

keycode is the two-character keyboard code for your location.

codepage is the three-digit code page that will be used.

*d:path***KEYBOARD.SYS** are the drive and the path to the KEYBOARD.SYS file.

An example list of **Country,*keycode,codepage*** follows: Australia,us,437/850; Belgium,be,437/850; Canadian-French,cf,863/850; Denmark,df,865/850; Finland,su, 437/850; France,fr,437/850; Germany,fr,437/850; Italy,it,437/850; Latin America,la,437/850; Netherlands,nl,437/850; Norway,no,865/850;

Portugal,po,860/850; Spain,sp,437/850; Sweden,sv,
437/850; Swiss-French,sf,437/850; Swiss-German,sg,
437/850; United Kingdom,uk,437/850; United States
(default),us,437/850.

Switches

/ID:*code*   Specifies the enhanced keyboard.

/E   Specifies that you are using an
                   enhanced keyboard. This switch is
                   useful for 8088/8086 computers.

Note

When KEYB is active, it reassigns some alphanumeric
characters to different keys and introduces new
characters. The new layout and characters vary among
the supported languages.

LABEL

(Volume Label)   *External*

Purpose

Creates, changes, or deletes a volume label for a disk.

Syntax

dc:pathc\LABEL d:volume_label

dc: is the name of the disk drive holding the command.

pathc is the path to the command.

d: is the name of the disk drive for which the label will
be changed.

volume_label is the new volume label for the disk.

LOADHIGH

(Load program in reserved memory)   *External*

Purpose

Loads device drivers or TSRs in reserved memory on an 80386sx, 80386, or 80486 computer.

Syntax

> *dc:pathc***LOADHIGH** *d:path***filename.ext**
> *prog_options*

dc:pathc are the drive and subdirectory on which LOADHIGH is located.

d:path is the location of the device driver or memory resident program.

filename.ext is the name of the device driver or memory resident program.

prog_options are any options that are required by **filename.ext**.

Notes

You must install HIMEM.SYS and EMM386.EXE as device drivers in CONFIG.SYS. You also must include the statement DOS=UMB in CONFIG.SYS.

Use this command for those programs you ordinarily use. You may want to include the LOADHIGH syntax in your AUTOEXEC.BAT file so that it is initiated each time you start your system.

MEM

(Display memory usage)   *External*

Purpose

Displays the amount of used and unused memory, allocated and open memory areas, and all programs currently in the system.

Syntax

> *dc:pathc***MEM** */PROGRAM /DEBUG*

dc:pathc are the disk drive and directory that hold the command.

Switches

/PROGRAM	Displays programs that are in memory, including the address, name, size, and type of each file for every program. Also shows current free memory.
/DEBUG	Displays programs that are in memory, including the address, name, size, and type of each file for every program. Also displays system device drivers and installed device drivers, as well as all unused memory.
/CLASSIFY	Displays programs in memory, including the size expressed in decimal and hexadecimal values. Displays statistics for conventional memory and upper memory (UMB).

Note

You can use MEM to display information on how memory is being used. MEM displays statistics for conventional memory and also for upper extended and expanded memory if the latter are available. You cannot specify /PROGRAM, /DEBUG, and /CLASSIFY at the same time.

MIRROR

(Protects against data loss)   *External*

Purpose

Saves information about a disk drive so that you can recover accidentally lost data.

Syntax

To save information about a drive and files that are deleted, use the form:

*dc:pathc*MIRROR *d1: d2: dn: /Tdrive-nnn /1*

To save information about a drive partition, use the form:

*dc:pathc*MIRROR *d1: d2: dn:* /PARTN

To quit tracking deleted files, use the form:

*dc:pathc*MIRROR /U

dc:pathc is the optional disk drive and subdirectory where MIRROR is located.

d1:, d2: and *dn:* are the disk drives for which you want to save information.

Switches

/Tdrive-nnn   Loads into memory a portion of MIRROR to keep track of files that you delete. *drive* is the mandatory disk drive for which deleted files are tracked. *entries* is an optional value from 1 to 999 that specifies the maximum number of files that are remembered when deleted. Default values are as follows:

• A 360K disk stores 25 entries.

• A 720K disk stores 50 entries.

- A 1.2M or 1.44M disk stores 75 entries.

- A 20M disk stores 101 entries.

- A 32M disk stores 202 entries.

- Disks over 32M store 303 entries.

/1   Keeps MIRROR from making a backup of the mirror file when the file is updated.

/PARTN   Makes a copy of the drive's partition table.

/U   Removes from memory the memory resident portion of MIRROR that keeps track of deleted files.

Notes

MIRROR creates a hidden file (MIRROR.FIL) on your hard disk that contains a copy of the root directory and file allocation table, which enables you to restore a drive if it is accidentally formatted.

Using the /T switch with MIRROR creates a hidden file called PCTRACKR.DEL, and leaves a portion of MIRROR in memory to track deleted files. PCTRACKR.DEL enables you to recover deleted files. To remove the memory resident portion of the program from memory, use the /U switch with MIRROR.

Using the /PARTN switch with MIRROR creates the file PARTNSAV.FIL on a diskette. This file contains information from the drives partition table initially created with FDISK. Label the diskette, and store it in a safe place.

Companion commands for MIRROR are UNFORMAT and UNDELETE.

The MIRROR command is not a replacement for doing proper backups of your hard disk!

MKDIR or MD

(Make directory)   *Internal*

Purpose

Creates a subdirectory.

Syntax

MKDIR *d:path***dirname**

or

MD *d:pat*h**dirname**

d: is the name of the disk drive for the subdirectory.

path is the valid path name for the path to the directory
that will hold the subdirectory.

dirname is the name of the subdirectory you are
creating.

MODE

(Set, Devices)   *External*

Purpose

Sets the mode of operation for the printer(s), the video
display, the keyboard, and the Asynchronous
Communications Adapter. Also controls code page
switching for the console and printer.

Syntax

To configure a parallel printer, use this syntax:

*dc:pathc***MODE LPT#:** *cpl, lpi, P*

or

*dc:pathc***MODE LPT#** *COLS=cpl LINES=lpi*
RETRY=ret

To set the display mode, use this syntax:

dc:pathc**MODE dt**

or

dc:pathc**MODE** *dt,* **s,** *T*

or

dc:pathc**MODE CON:** *COLS=col LINES=line*

To configure a serial port, use this syntax:

dc:pathc**MODE COMn: baud,** *parity, databits, stopbits, P*

or

dc:pathc**MODE COMn** *BAUD=baud PARITY=parity* **DATA=***databits* **STOP=***stopbits* **RETRY=***ret*

To redirect the parallel port to the serial port, use this syntax:

dc:pathc**MODE LPT#: = COMn**

To set Code Pages, use this syntax:

dc:pathc**MODE device CODEPAGE PREPARE =((codepage,** *codepage, . . .) dp:pathp*\ **pagefile.***ext***)**
or

dc:pathc**MODE device CODEPAGE SELECT =** **codepage**

or

dc:pathc**MODE device CODEPAGE REFRESH**

or

dc:pathc**MODE device CODEPAGE */STATUS***

To set the keyboards repeat rate, use this syntax:

dc:pathc**MODE CON:** *RATE=rate DELAY=delay*

To view the status of a device, use this syntax:

*dc:pathc***MODE** *device* /**STATUS**

dc: is the name of the disk drive holding the command.

pathc is the path to the command.

#: is the printer number (1, 2, or 3). The colon is optional.

cpl are the characters per line (80 or 132).

lpi are the lines per inch (6 or 8).

P specifies continuous retries on timeout errors.

ret specifies one of the following retry actions: E returns an error if the port is busy; P continues retrying; B returns busy if the port is busy; R returns ready if the port is busy; and N is no retry action.

dt is display type, which may be one of the following values: **40**, **80**, **BW40**, **BW80**, **CO40**, **CO80**, or **MONO**.

s shifts the graphics display right or left one character.

T requests alignment of the graphics display screen with a one-line test pattern.

col is the number of columns to display on the screen.

lines is the number of lines to display on the screen. This is only applicable for an EGA (25 or 43) or VGA (25, 43 or 50) display.

n: is the adapter number (1 or 2). The colon after the number is optional.

baud is the baud rate (110, 150, 300, 1200, 2400, 4800, or 9600).

parity is the parity checking (None, Odd, or Even).

databits is the number of data bits (7 or 8).

stopbits is the number of stop bits (1 or 2).

P represents continuous retries on timeout errors.

#: is the parallel printer number (1, 2, or 3). The colon is optional.

n is the asynchronous Communications Adapter number (1 or 2).

device is the name of the device for which code page(s) will be chosen. Valid devices include the following:

- **CON:**, which is the console.

- **PRN:**, which is the first parallel printer.

- **LPT#:**, which is any parallel printer (# is 1, 2, or 3).

codepage is the number of the code page(s) to be used with the device. The numbers are as follows:

- 437 United States

- 850 Multilingual

- 860 Portuguese

- 863 Canadian-French

- 865 Nordic

. . . represents additional code pages

dp: is the name of the disk drive that contains the code page (font) information.

pathp is the path to the file containing the code page (font) information.

pagefile.*ext* is the name of the file containing the code page (font) information. Currently, the provided code page files are as follows:

4201.CPI	IBM Proprinter, Printer XL
4208.CPI	IBM Proprinter X24, Printer XL24
5202.CPI	IBM Quietwriter III printer
EGA.CPI	EGA type displays or IBM PS/2
LCD.CPI	IBM Convertible Liquid Crystal Display

rate is the speed, from 1 to 32, at which characters repeat. The speed varies from 2 cps to 30 cps.

delay is the number from 1 through 4 that specifies .25, .5, .75, or 1 second delay before repeating begins.

Switch

/STATUS   Displays the *status* of the device's setting.

MORE ══════════════════════════════

(More output filter)   *External*

Purpose

Displays one screen of information from the standard input device and pauses and displays the message - More - . When you press any key, MORE displays the next screen of information.

Syntax

dc:pathc\MORE

dc: is the name of the disk drive holding the command.

pathc is the path to the command.

Examples

MORE <TEST.TXT

MORE displays a screenful of information from the file TEST.TXT, then displays the prompt - More - at the bottom of the screen and waits for a keystroke. When you press a key, MORE continues this process until all information has been displayed.

DIR | SORT | MORE

MORE displays the sorted output of the directory command.

NLSFUNC

(National language support) **External**

Purpose

Provides support for extended country information in MS-DOS and allows use of the CHCP command.

Syntax

dc:pathc\NLSFUNC d:path\filename.ext

dc: is the name of the disk drive holding the command.

pathc is the path to the command.

d: is the name of the disk drive holding the country information file.

path is the path to the country information file.

filename.*ext* is the name of the file holding the country information. With DOS 5, this information is contained in the file COUNTRY.SYS.

PATH

(Set directory search order) **Internal**

Purpose

Tells MS-DOS to search the specified directories on the specified drives if a program or batch file is not found in the current directory.

Syntax

PATH *d1:path1;d2:path2;d3:path3;. . .*

d1:, *d2:*, and *d3:* are valid disk drive names.

path1, *path2*, and *path3* are valid path names to the commands you want to run while in any directory.

. . . are additional disk drives and path names.

Note that you are limited to 127 characters.

PRINT

(Background printing)　　　　　　**External**

Purpose

Prints a list of files while the computer performs other tasks.

Syntax

$dc:pathc\$**PRINT** $/D:device$ $/B:bufsiz$ $/M:maxtick$
$/Q:maxfiles$ $/S:timeslice$ $/U:busytick$
$d1:path1\filename1.ext1$ $/P/T/C$
$d2:path2\filename2.ext2$ $/P/T/C. . .$

dc: is the name of the disk drive holding the command.

pathc is the path to the command.

d1: and *d2:* are valid disk drive names.

path1 and *path2* are valid path names to the files for printing.

filename1.ext1 and *filename2.ext2* are names of the files you want to print. Wildcards are allowed.

. . . represents additional file names in the form of *dx:pathx\filenamex.extx* and are valid file specifications.

Switches

Switches used when you first issue PRINT are as follows:

/B:bufsize	The size of the buffer in bytes.
/D:device	The *device* to use.
/M:maxtick	The *maximum* number of clock ticks to use.
/Q:maxfiles	The maximum number of files to *queue*.
/U:busytick	The number of clock ticks to wait for the printer.

/S:timeslice	The number of times per *second* that PRINT can print (number of *timeslices*).

Switches used any time you issue PRINT are as follows:

/T	Terminates printing of all files.
/C	Cancels the printing of the file.
/P	Prints this file.

PROMPT

(Set the System Prompt)   *Internal*

Purpose

Customizes the MS-DOS system prompt (the A> or A prompt).

Syntax

PROMPT *promptstring*

promptstring is the text to be used for the new system prompt.

Rules

The following rules apply to PROMPT:

- Any text entered for *promptstring* becomes the new system prompt. You may enter special characters with the meta-strings. The new system prompt stays in effect until you restart MS-DOS or reissue the PROMPT command.

- To see the text of PROMPT after it has been set, use the SET command.

Meta-Strings

A *meta-string* is a group of characters transformed into another character or characters. To use certain characters (for example, the < or > I/O redirection symbols), you must enter the appropriate meta-string to place the desired character(s) in your *promptstring*. Otherwise, MS-DOS immediately attempts to interpret the character.

All meta-strings begin with the dollar sign ($) and consist of two characters, including the $. The following list contains meta-string characters and their meanings:

Character	Produces
$	$, the dollar sign.
_ (underscore)	New line (moves to the first position of the next line).
b	|, the vertical bar.
d	The date, same as the DATE command.
e	The escape character, CHR$(27).
g	>, the greater-than character.
h	The backspace character, CHR$(8), which erases the previous character.
l	<, the less-than character.
n	The current disk drive.
p	The current disk drive and path, including the current directory.
q	=, the equal sign.
t	The time, same as the TIME command.
v	The version number of MS-DOS.
Any other	Nothing or null; the character is ignored.

Examples

To change the prompt to display the current drive, path, and a greater than sign (C:\DOS>), type

PROMPT pg

To change the prompt to display the date on one line and the drive and path in brackets on the second line, type

PROMPT d_[$p]

To reset the prompt to the default (C>), type

PROMPT

QBASIC

(Basic Interpreter)   *External*

Purpose

Loads the BASIC interpreter into memory for BASIC programming.

Syntax

*dc:pathc***QBASIC** *d:path\filename.ext /H /NOHI /B
/EDITOR /G /MBF /RUN*

dc:pathc are the drive and subdirectory on which QBASIC is located.

d:path is the optional location of the BASIC program to load into memory.

filename.ext is the name of the BASIC program.

Switches

/H	Changes the display mode to view QBASIC with the maximum number of lines on the screen.
/NOHI	Enables QBASIC to work with monitors that do not support the high intensity video.

/B	Places QBASIC in Black and White mode.
/EDITOR	Starts the editor in nonprogramming mode.
/RUN	Loads and runs the program.
/G	Enables a CGA monitor to update quickly. You should not use this switch if "snow" appears on the screen.
/MBF	Enables the QBASIC statements CVS, CVD, MKS$, and MKD$ to use the Microsoft Binary Format for numbers.

RECOVER

(Recover files or disk directory)   *External*

Purpose

Recovers a file that contains bad sectors or a file from a disk with a damaged directory.

Syntax

To recover a file, type

   *dc:pathc***RECOVER** *d:path\filename.ext*

To recover a disk with a damaged directory, type

   *dc:pathc***RECOVER d:**

dc: is the name of the disk drive holding the command.

pathc is the path to the command.

d: is the name of the disk drive holding the damaged file or diskette.

path is the path to the directory holding the file to be recovered.

filename.ext is the file to be recovered. Wildcards are allowed, but only the first file that matches the wildcard file name is RECOVERed.

RENAME or REN

(Rename file)   *Internal*

Purpose

Changes the name of the disk file(s).

Syntax

RENAME *d:path*filename1.*ext1* filename2.*ext2*

or

REN *d:path*filename1.*ext1* filename2.*ext2*

d: is the name of the disk drive holding the file(s) to be renamed.

path is the path to the file(s) to be renamed.

filename1.*ext1* is the current name of the file. Wildcards are allowed.

filename2.*ext2* is the new name for the file. Wildcards are allowed.

REPLACE

(Replace/update files)   *External*

Purpose

Selectively replaces files with matching names from one disk to another. Selectively adds files from one disk to another.

Syntax

> dc:pathc**REPLACE** ds:paths\\filenames.exts
> dd:pathd /A/P/R/S/W/U

dc: is the name of the disk drive holding the command.

pathc is the path to the command.

ds: is the name of the disk drive holding the replacement files.

paths is the path to the replacement files.

filenames.*exts* is the name of the replacement files. Wildcards are allowed.

dd: is the name of the disk drive holding the replacement files.

pathd is the path to the replacement files.

Terms

The file that will be added to or that will replace another file is the *source* represented by an *s* in the name (*ds:paths*filenames.*exts*).

The file that will be replaced or the disk and directory that will contain the added file is the des*tination*, represented by the letter *d* (*dd:pathd*). MS-DOS refers to this as the *target*.

Switches

/A   Adds files from sources that do not exist on the destination.

/P   Prompts and asks whether the file should be replaced or added to the destination.

/R   Replaces read-only files also.

/S   Replaces files in the current directory and allows subdirectories beneath this directory.

/W   Waits for the source diskette to be inserted.

/U   Replaces only those files of a date and time earlier than the source files.

RESTORE

(Restore backed up files)   *External*

Purpose

Restores one or more backup files from a diskette or
hard disk onto another diskette or hard disk. This
command complements the BACKUP command.

Syntax

RESTORE d1: *d2:path\filename.ext /S /P /M /N
/B:date /A:date /L:time /E:time /D*

d1: is the name of the disk drive holding the backup
file(s).

d2: is the disk drive to receive the restored file(s).

path is the path name of the path to the directory to
receive the restored file(s).

filename.ext is the name of the file you want to restore.
Wildcards are allowed.

Switches

/S	Restores files in the directory specified and all other subdirectories below it. This switch is identical to BACKUP's /S switch.
/P	Prompts and asks whether a file should be restored if it is marked as read-only or has been changed since the last backup.
/N	Restores all files that no longer exist on the destination. This switch is like the /M switch, but /N processes only the files deleted from the destination since the backup set was made.

/M   Restores all files modified or deleted
              since the backup set was made. This
              switch is like the /N switch because
              /M processes files that no longer
              exist on the destination, but /M also
              restores files that have been
              modified since the last backup.

/A:date   Restores all files created or modified
              on or after the *date*. The format of
              date is the same as the /B switch.

/B:date   Restores all files created or modified
              on or before the *date*.

/L:time   Restores all files modified at or later
              than the specified *time*. The form of
              time is *hh:mm:ss*, where *hh* is the
              hour; *mm*, the minutes; and *ss*, the
              seconds.

E/:time   Restores all files modified at or
              earlier than the specified *time*.

/D   Displays files that match spec
              without restoring files.

RMDIR or RD

(Remove directory)   *Internal*

Purpose

Removes a subdirectory.

Syntax

RMDIR d:path

or

RD *d:* path

d: is the name of the drive holding the subdirectory.

path is the name of the path to the subdirectory. The last
path name is the subdirectory you want to delete.

SET

(Set/show environment)   *Internal*

Purpose

Sets or shows the system environment.

Syntax

To display the environment, type

SET

To add to or alter the environment, type

SET name=*string*

name is the name of the string you want to add to the
environment.

string is the information you want to store in the
environment.

Term

The *environment* is an area in RAM memory reserved
for alphanumeric information that may be examined and
used by MS-DOS commands or user programs.

SETVER

(Emulate previous DOS versions)   *External*

Purpose

Sets a specific DOS version to be emulated with a
program file.

Syntax

To add a program to the version table, use the form:

dc:pathc\SETVER d: **filename.ext dosver**

To remove a program from the version table, use the form:

dc:pathc\SETVER **filename.ext** */DELETE*

To view the version table, use the form:

dc:pathc\SETVER

dc:pathc are the drive and subdirectory path in which SETVER is located.

d: is the drive that contains the DOS system files.

filename.ext is the program file to add to the version table.

dosver is a valid version of DOS previous to DOS 5 (4.01, 4.00, 3.30, 3.20, and so on.)

Switches

/DELETE	Removes a program and its associated DOS version from the version table.
/QUIET	Displays no messages. Works with /DELETE only.

Note

SETVER enables programs requiring specific DOS versions to operate with DOS V5. When you use SETVER, the current version table is affected. The change is not active until you restart DOS, however. Specifying a file that is already in the version table will modify the files settings.

SHARE

(Check shared files)   *External*

Purpose

Enables MS-DOS support for file and record locking.

Syntax

*dc:pathc*SHARE */F:name_space /L:numlocks*

dc: is the name of the disk drive holding the command.

pathc is the path to the command.

Switches

/F:name_space	Sets the amount of memory space (name_space bytes large) used for file sharing.
/L:numlocks	Sets the maximum number (numlocks) of file/record locks to use.

Rules

The following rules apply to the SHARE command:

- If you do not specify the */F* switch, *name_space* is set to 2,048 bytes. Each open file uses 11 bytes plus its full file specification (disk drive name, path name, and file name). The 2,048 bytes can contain 27 files that use all 63 characters available for the full file name.

- If you do not specify the */L* switch, a default of 20 simultaneous file locks is allowed.

- When SHARE is loaded, MS-DOS checks each file for file and record locks during the opening, reading, and writing of the file.

- SHARE should be loaded only once after MS-DOS has started. If you attempt to load SHARE again, MS-DOS displays an error message.

- SHARE normally increases the size of MS-DOS by approximately 4,900 bytes. If the number of locks (*/L* switch) or memory space (*/F* switch) is increased or decreased, the size of MS-DOS also increases or decreases proportionately.

- The only way to remove SHARE is to restart MS-DOS.

- If you have not given the FCBS command in your
  CONFIG.SYS file, SHARE adjusts the file control
  block (FCB) table as if the command FCBS = 16,8
  were given.

Note

You use SHARE when two or more programs or
processes share the files of a single computer, whether
via a network or a multitasking program such as
Windows 3.0. After SHARE is loaded, MS-DOS checks
each file for locks whenever it is opened, read, or
written. If a file has been opened for exclusive use, a
second attempt to open the file produces an error. If one
program locks a portion of a file, another program
attempting to read, write, or read and write the locked
portion creates an error.

═SORT

(Sort string filter)   *External*

Purpose

Reads lines from the standard input device, performs an
ASCII sort of the lines, and then writes the lines to the
standard output device. The sorting may be in ascending
or descending order and may start at any column in the
line.

Syntax

> *dc:pathc*SORT */R /+c*

dc: is the name of the disk drive holding the command.

pathc is the path to the command.

Switches

/R   Sorts in reverse order. Thus, the letter Z comes
         first, and the letter A comes last.

/+c   Starts sorting with column number c.

Examples

SORT <WORDS.TXT

SORT sorts the lines in the file WORDS.TXT and displays the sorted lines on the video screen.

SORT <WORDS.TXT /R

SORT sorts in reverse order the lines in the file WORDS.TXT and displays the lines on the video screen.

SORT /+8 <WORDS.TXT

SORT starts sorting at the eighth character in each line of WORDS.TXT and displays the output on the video display.

DIR | SORT /+14

SORT displays the directory information sorted by file size. (The file size starts in the 14th column.) Unfortunately, other lines, such as the volume label, are also sorted starting at the 14th column.

SUBST

(Substitute path name) *External*

Purpose

Creates an alias disk drive name for a subdirectory; used principally with programs that do not use path names.

Syntax

To establish an alias, type

dc:pathc\SUBST d1: d2:pathname

To delete an alias, type

dc:pathc\SUBST d1: /D

To see the current aliases, type

dc:pathc\SUBST

dc: is the name of the disk drive holding the command.

pathc is the path to the command.

d1: is a valid disk drive name that becomes the alias (or nickname). **d1:** may be a nonexistent disk drive.

d2:pathname is a valid disk drive name and directory path that will be nicknamed **d1:**.

Switch

/D   Deletes the alias.

Examples

SUBST E: C:\BIN

When you use disk drive name E, the directory C:\BIN actually is used.

SUBST F: C:LETTERS

Drive F is substituted for the directory C:\WORDS \LETTERS. Because the current directory of drive C was \WORDS, MS-DOS found LETTERS as the subdirectory of WORDS. MS-DOS adds \WORDS\ to the alias.

SUBST

Shows the current aliases. SUBST displays.

```
E: => C:\BIN

F: => C:\WORDS\LETTERS
```

SUBST F: /D

The alias **F**: is deleted. Afterward, the use of **F**: produces an error message from MS-DOS.

SYS

(Place the operating system on the disk) External

Purpose

Places a copy of MS-DOS on the specified diskette or hard disk.

Syntax

*dc:pathc*SYS d1: *d2:*

dc: is the name of the disk drive holding the command.

pathc is the path to the command.

d1: is the disk drive to receive the copy of MS-DOS.

d2: is the disk drive that contains the copy of MS-DOS.

Rules

The following rules apply to the SYS command:

- You must specify the name of the disk drive to receive a copy of MS-DOS.

- The destination disk must contain no data or have been formatted with the */S* or */B* option previously.

Note

The SYS command places a copy of IO.SYS and MSDOS.SYS on the targeted disk. To make the disk bootable (able to load and execute the disk operating system), you must also copy COMMAND.COM.

TIME

(Set/show the time)   *Internal*

Purpose

Sets and shows the system time.

Syntax

>   TIME *hh:mm:ss.xx*

hh is a one- or two-digit number for hours (0 to 23).

mm is a one- or two-digit number for minutes (0 to 60).

ss is a one- or two-digit number for seconds (0 to 60).

xx is a one- or two-digit number for hundredths of a second (0 to 99).

Note

Depending on the setting of the country code in your CONFIG.SYS file, a comma may be the separator between seconds and hundredths of seconds.

TREE

(Display all directories)   ***External***

Purpose

Displays all the subdirectories on a disk and optionally displays all the files in each directory.

Syntax

>   *dc:pathc*TREE *d: /F /A /?*

dc:pathc are the disk drive and the directory that hold the command.

d: is the disk drive holding the disk you want to examine.

Switches

/F   Displays all files in the directories.

/A   Uses ASCII characters rather than linedraw characters to display the connection of subdirectories.

TYPE

(Type file on screen)   *Internal*

Purpose

Displays the contents of the file on the screen.

Syntax

TYPE *d:path***filename**.*ext*

d: is the name of the disk drive holding the file to TYPE.

path\ is the MS-DOS path to the file.

filename.*ext* is the name of the file to TYPE. Wildcards are not permitted.

UNDELETE

(Restore a deleted file)   *External*

Purpose

Restores deleted files.

Syntax

To list files that may be undeleted, use the form:

dc:pathc\UNDELETE *dd:pathd\filenamed.extd*
/LIST

To restore individual files using the delete tracking file created with MIRROR, use the form:

dc:pathc\UNDELETE *dd:pathd\filenamed.extd*
/DT

To restore individual files if a delete tracking file does not exist, use the form:

dc:pathc\UNDELETE *dd:pathd\filenamed.extd*
/DOS

To restore all files, using the delete tracking file if one exists, use the form:

>   *dc:pathc*UNDELETE *dd:pathd\filenamed.extd*
>   /ALL

dc:pathc is the drive and subdirectory where UNDELETE is located.

dd:pathd\filenamed.extd is the drive and subdirectory location of the file *filenamed.extd* to restore.

Switches

/LIST	Displays the files that may be recovered. If you specify a file, or files to be recovered, the list is limited by the file name.
/DT	Specifies UNDELETE to restore files based on the information in the delete tracking file created by the MIRROR command.
/DOS	Specifies UNDELETE to restore files based on the directory contents. You must confirm each file before it is restored. If a delete tracking file exists, it is ignored.
/ALL	Recovers all files without prompting. UNDELETE will use the delete tracking file, if one exists. Otherwise UNDELETE will use the standard DOS directory. If the DOS directory is used, then the missing first character will be replaced by #. If a second filename conflicts with an already-restored file, then another character will replace the #.

Note

When a file is deleted, the first character in the file name is removed. If you undelete using the \DOS switch, you are prompted to specify the actual character that should replace the missing first character. If you use the /ALL switch, and a delete tracking file does not exist, each deleted file is restored without prompting.

UNFORMAT

(Recover a formatted disk) *External*

Purpose

Reconstructs a formatted diskette.

Syntax

To test or recover erased files or a formatted disk, use the form:

*dc:pathc*UNFORMAT *d1:* /J /P /L /TEST

To recover a disk whose partition has been lost, use the form:

*dc:pathc*UNFORMAT /PARTN

dc:pathc are the drive and subdirectory on which UNFORMAT is located.

d1: is the drive on which UNFORMAT should act.

Switches

/J   Tests the files created by MIRROR to see whether they are up-to-date with information on the disk. Does not unformat the disk.

/L   Lists on-screen all files and subdirectories that UNFORMAT finds. When used with the /PARTN switch, the partition table is displayed on the screen.

/P   Prints a list of all files and subdirectories that UNFORMAT finds. When used with the /PARTN switch, the partition table is printed.

/TEST	Performs a simulated unformat of the disk.
/PARTN	Restores a hard disk's partition table with the PARTNSAV.FIL created by MIRROR.
/U	Unformats without using mirror file.

Notes

UNFORMAT attempts to recover a formatted disk using the files created by MIRROR or the file created by a safe format.

To use UNFORMAT, you should format a diskette using FORMAT /S, and transfer the UNFORMAT.EXE, AUTOEXEC.BAT, and CONFIG.SYS to the diskette. Also, transfer to the diskette any device drivers that are necessary for the computer's operation. You may need to edit AUTOEXEC.BAT and CONFIG.SYS to read files from the diskette.

Before using UNFORMAT, use UNFORMAT with the /J or /TEST switches. This procedure enables you to determine whether your MIRROR files are up-to-date, or if the UNFORMAT will be performed to your expectations.

The UNFORMAT command is not a replacement for proper backups of your hard disk!

VER

(Display version number)   *Internal*

Purpose

Shows the MS-DOS version number on the video display.

Syntax

VERIFY

(Set/show disk verification)   *Internal*

Purpose

Sets the computer to check the accuracy of data written
to the disk(s) to ensure that information is properly
recorded, and shows whether the data has been checked.

Syntax

To show the verify status, use the form:

VERIFY

To set the verify status, use the form:

VERIFY ON

or

VERIFY OFF

Rules

The following rules apply to the VERIFY command:

- VERIFY accepts only one of two parameters: ON or
  OFF.

- Once VERIFY is ON, it remains on until one of the
  following occurs:

  A VERIFY OFF is issued.

  A SET VERIFY system call turns off the command.

  MS-DOS is restarted.

Note

VERIFY does not affect any other MS-DOS operation.
Although VERIFY assures the integrity of the recorded
data, the trade-off is in extra time needed to verify the
data.

VOL

(Display volume label)   *Internal*

Purpose

Displays the volume label of the disk, if the label exists.

Syntax

VOL *d:*

d: is the name of the disk drive whose label you want to
display.

XCOPY

(Extended COPY)   *External*

Purpose

Selectively copies files from one or more subdirectories.

Syntax

*dc:pathc***XCOPY** *ds:paths\filenames.exts*
dd:pathd\filenamed.extd /A /D:date
/E /M /P /S /V /W

dc: is the name of the disk drive holding the command.

pathc is the path to the command.

ds: is the name of the disk drive holding the files to be
copied.

paths is the path to the files to be copied.

filenames.exts is the name of the file(s) to be copied.
Wildcards are allowed.

dd: is the name of the disk drive that will receive the
copied files.(MS-DOS refers to it as the target).

pathd is the path that will receive the copied files.

filenamed.extd is the name to be given to the copied
files. Wildcards are allowed.

Switches

/V	Verifies that the files have been copied correctly (identical to COPY's /V switch).
/W	Waits until the disk has been changed. XCOPY prompts you to change diskettes before it searches for the files to copy.
/P	Pauses and asks for confirmation before copying each file.
/S	Copies the files in the source directory and all files in subsequent subdirectories. This option is identical to BACKUP's and RESTORE's /S switch.
/E	When given with the /S switch, causes XCOPY to create empty subdirectories on the destination if the subdirectory on the source is empty. If you do not give the /E switch, /S ignores empty directories.
/A	Copies files with archive flags set to on (the file has been created or modified since the last running of BACKUP or XCOPY). /A does not reset the file's archive flag.
/M	Copies files with archive flags set to on (the file has been created or modified since the last running of BACKUP or XCOPY). /M resets the file's archive flag.
/D:*date*	Copies files created or modified since *date*. This option is identical to BACKUP's /D switch.

BATCH FILES

A batch file provides a shortcut for executing one or many MS-DOS commands. When you type just the name of a batch file, the file executes each line as if you had entered the line from the keyboard.

Batch files can automate long or repetitive instructions. The chance of mistyping a command is reduced, and lengthy tasks can be started and left to run unattended.

You can view writing batch file as a way of programming in MS-DOS. This section indicates the procedure for creating batch files, explains the batch subcommands, and gives examples of batch files you can use.

Creating Batch Files

You can create batch files by using COPY CON, any word processor capable of creating text files (most can), or a text editor (including the MS-DOS EDIT editor). COPY CON is not recommended for the longer examples, however, because it is not easy to correct typing errors.

If you use a word processor, use the programmer or nondocument mode, or save the file as an ASCII file. The normal mode of many word processors stores the characters you type in a code that MS-DOS may not understand. If your word processing program does not distinguish between documents and nondocuments, use the following method to create a test batch file:

1. Type a simple batch file like those explained in this section. Each line of the file must be a single, executable MS-DOS command. Avoid underlining, bold, and other special formatting. Make sure that no hard return or other symbols appear on-screen.

2. Save the batch file with a file extension of BAT; then try to run it at the MS-DOS prompt.

If a `Bad Command or File Name` message appears, consult your word processor's manual. Look up ASCII files to see how the program stores files in ASCII or nondocument mode. If no information is available, contact the software publisher to find out how to write batch files with the program.

The batch files given in this section are typed in all capital letters. MS-DOS accepts lowercase letters except in special cases that are pointed out in the text.

Rules for Creating Batch Files

The following rules apply when you create batch files:

- The batch file's root name can range from one to eight characters in length and must conform to the DOS rules for creating file names. You must use the file name extension .BAT.

- A batch file should not have the same root name as that of a program file (a file ending with .COM and .EXE) in the current directory. Nor should you use an internal MS-DOS command, such as COPY or DATE, as a root name. If you use one of these root names to name a batch file, and then try to run the batch file, MS-DOS will execute the program or the command instead.

- You can enter any valid MS-DOS system-level commands. You also can use the parameter markers (%0-%9) or environmental variables by enclosing the variable name in percent signs (such as %COMSPEC%).

- You can enter any valid batch subcommand.

- To use the percent sign (%) for a file name in a command, enter the percent symbol twice. For example, to use a file called A100%.TXT, you enter A100%%.TXT. This rule does not apply to the parameter markers (0%-9%) or environmental variables.

- You can suppress the display of any line from the batch file if an @ is the first nonspace character on the line.

Executing Batch Files

You execute a batch file by entering the batch-file name at the MS-DOS prompt, using the following syntax:

*dc:pathc***filename** *parameters*

dc: is the name of the disk drive that holds the batch file.

pathc is the path to the batch file.

filename is the batch file's root name.

parameters are the parameters the batch file uses.

Rules for Executing Batch Files

The following rules apply when you execute batch files:

- To invoke a batch file, simply type its root name. For example, to invoke the batch file OFTEN.BAT, type **OFTEN**, and then press **Enter**.

- MS-DOS executes each command one line at a time. The specified parameters are substituted for the markers when the command is used.

- MS-DOS recognizes a maximum of ten parameters. If you do not want to be limited to this number of parameters, use the SHIFT subcommand.

- If MS-DOS encounters an incorrectly phrased batch subcommand, it displays a Syntax error message, and then continues executing the remaining commands in the batch file.

- To stop a running batch file, press **Ctrl-Break**. MS-DOS displays this message:

  ```
  Terminate batch job (Y/N)?_
  ```

  If you press **Y**, the rest of the commands are ignored and the system prompt appears. If you press **N**, MS-DOS skips the current command but continues to process the other commands in the file.

- MS-DOS remembers which directory holds the batch file. Your batch file may cause the current directory to change at any time.

- MS-DOS remembers which diskette holds the batch file, and you can change diskettes at any time. MS-DOS prompts you to insert the diskette that holds the batch file, if necessary.

- You can make MS-DOS execute a second batch file immediately after the first one is finished. Simply enter the name of the second batch file as the last command in the first batch file. You also can execute a second batch file within the first batch file and return to the first batch file by using the CALL subcommand.

- Batch subcommands are valid only for batch files. With the exception of FOR..IN..DO, you cannot execute batch file subcommands as normal MS-DOS commands.

- Although you cannot redirect the input or output of a batch file, you can use redirection in the lines within a batch file.

- When MS-DOS executes the AUTOEXEC.BAT file after the computer boots, the system does not automatically request the date and time. To get the current date and time, you must put the DATE and TIME commands in the AUTOEXEC.BAT file.

Starting a Program with a Batch File

You probably use the same programs each day. To start each program, you must type several DOS commands. To speed up this process, you can create a batch file. Suppose that you want to create a batch file that starts Lotus 1-2-3. Notice the following batch file that you create and place on your search path:

```
CD\123
123
XCOPY C:\DATA\123 A:/M
CD\
```

Select a name appropriate to the batch file action. In this case 123.BAT. To start the batch file, type 123 and press Enter.

Creating a Batch File Using DOSKEY

DOSKEY is a terminate, stay-resident program that manages the commands you type at the command line. The number of commands DOSKEY remembers depends on the amount of memory you allocate to DOSKEY.

After you type several commands at the command line, you can reuse each command by pressing the up-arrow key to recall a past command. When you use the /HISTORY switch with DOSKEY, all the commands that DOSKEY can remember are listed on-screen. Using redirection, the commands can be saved to a file.

Suppose that each day you use the BACKUP command to copy files from the C:\LTR directory to backup disks after you erase all backup files created by your word processor. From the command line, start DOSKEY by typing

DOSKEY

and press Enter.

Next, type the commands you use on a daily basis. For example

DEL C:\LTR*.BAK
BACKUP C:\LTR A:

To save these commands to a batch file called BACKLTR.BAT, type

DOSKEY /HISTORY > BACKLTR.BAT

The history of the two commands is redirected to become the contents of a file, BACKLTR.BAT.

Using CLS to Clear the Screen

Running several DOS utilities in a row may leave information on-screen and may make it difficult for you to find this information you need. The CLS command removes unwanted information from the screen. The CLS command often is included in a batch file as follows:

```
ECHO OFF
CLS
```

The screen clears and ECHO OFF suppresses the display
of commands.

Defining Parameters

The information you type after the command is called a
parameter. Within a batch file, you can define up to 10
parameters. You define a parameter within the batch file
by using a *variable marker*. A variable is a percent sign
(%) followed by a number from 0 to 9. Variables are
called markers, replaceable parameters, or arguments.

Examples

Consider the file MOVE.BAT. This batch file copies a
file to a designated subdirectory and then erases the
original file:

```
@ECHO OFF
COPY %1 %2 /V
DEL C:\%1
```

Suppose that you type the following command line:

```
MOVE C:\DATA\123\SCHEDULE.WK1
C:\DATA\HOURS
```

The batch file MOVE.BAT begins executing and each
parameter marker is replaced by the respective
parameter. The batch file executes as follows:

```
@ECHO OFF
COPY C:\DATA\123\SCHEDULE.WK1
C:\DATA\HOURS/V
DEL C:\DATA\123\SCHEDULE.WK1
```

SCHEDULE.WK1 is copied from C:\DATA\123 to
C:\DATA\HOURS and verified as it is copied.

You can modify MOVE.BAT with the SHIFT command
so that you can specify the movement of several files on
one line. The new MOVE.BAT file follows:

```
@ECHO OFF
:LOOP
IF "%2" =.=""GOTO END
ECHO Moving %1 to %2
COPY %1 %2 /V
DEL %1
SHIFT
SHIFT
GOTO LOOP
:END
```

The syntax to use this batch file is

> MOVE source1 destination1 source2 destination2...

Notice that you can type pairs of source and destination files. The batch file uses IF to make sure that you entered parameters. If the second parameter (%2) is empty, the batch file goes to END (the batch file quits). If the second parameter is not empty, the source file is copied to the destination and then deleted.

The two SHIFT commands throw away the first pair of source and destination parameters. The second pair of parameters become %1 and %2, respectively. The batch file returns to the label :LOOP, and the entire process starts again.

Counting Parameters

A batch file has 10 possible parameters: %0 through %9. The first parameter is parameter number 0 and is designated as %0 in batch files. The parameter %0 signifies the name of the batch file you typed at the MS-DOS prompt.

The remaining items on the line are parameters 1 through 9. The first word after the batch file name is parameter number 1, %1 in the file. The second word is %2, and the ninth item on the line is %9. Each word on the line is separated from the next by a space, comma, colon, semicolon, single quotation mark, or equal sign.

When you use replaceable parameters, remember to start with %1, not with %0.

Although MS-DOS restricts you to parameters 0 to 9 within a batch file, a command line can have many parameters within its 127-character limit. See the explanation of the SHIFT subcommand to learn how to trick MS-DOS into using the other arguments.

Using Batch File Commands

You can use any valid MS-DOS command in a batch file. MS-DOS also has a set of commands specifically for use in batch files: the batch subcommands. The batch subcommands for V5 follow.

Command	*Operation*
@	Suppresses the display of a line on-screen.
CALL	Runs another batch file and then returns to the original batch file.
ECHO	Turns the display of batch commands on or off and displays a message on the screen.
FOR..IN..DO	Allows the use of the same batch command for several files.
GOTO	Jumps to the line after a label in the batch file.
IF	Allows conditional execution of a command.
PAUSE	Halts processing until a key is pressed and optionally displays a message.
REM	Displays a message on the screen.

SHIFT   Shifts the command line
                         parameters one parameter to the
                         left.

CALL ═══════════════════════════════

Batch Subcommand

Purpose

Runs a second batch file, and then returns control to the
first batch file.

Syntax

CALL *dc:pathc*filename *parameters*

dc: is the name of the disk drive that holds the called
batch file.

pathc is the path to the called batch file.

filename is the root name of the called batch file.

parameters are the parameters the batch file will use.

Notes

Use the CALL command to run a second batch file from
another batch file. When the second batch file is
finished, MS-DOS continues processing the remaining
commands in the first batch file.

If you do not use CALL to run the second batch file,
MS-DOS concludes batch-file processing when the
second file finishes. MS-DOS does not usually return to
the first batch file.

ECHO

Batch Subcommand

Purpose

Displays a message and either permits or inhibits the display of batch commands and messages by other batch subcommands as MS-DOS executes these subcommands.

Syntax

To display a message, type

ECHO *message*

message is the text of the message to be displayed on the video screen.

To display a blank line separating more than one *message*, use a period directly after ECHO

ECHO.

To turn off the display of commands and messages by other batch commands, type

ECHO OFF

To turn on the display of commands and messages, type

ECHO ON

To see the status of ECHO, type

ECHO

Example

The following example uses the ECHO command to display messages:

ECHO OFF
ECHO To run this program, make sure
ECHO the disk containing BASICA is
ECHO in drive A and the disk labeled
ECHO CONTRACTS is in drive B.
ECHO.

    ECHO (If you need to exit at this time,
    ECHO hold down the Ctrl key and press
    ECHO the Break key. When the system
    ECHO asks you whether you want to
    ECHO "Terminate batch job (Y/N)?"
    ECHO press Y. The batch file will stop.)

The first command, ECHO OFF, is the "noise suppressor." ECHO OFF suppresses the *echoing* (displaying) of any batch commands on-screen as these commands are executed. However, ECHO OFF does not turn off messages displayed by another ECHO command. ECHO OFF turns off REM statements but not other ECHO statements. Running the preceding chunk of a batch file produces the following display:

```
C>ECHO OFF
To run this program, make sure
the disk containing BASICA is
in drive A and the disk labeled CONTRACTS
is in drive B.

(If you need to exit at this time,
hold down the Ctrl key and press
the Break key. When the system
asks you whether you want to
"Terminate batch job (Y/N)?"
press Y. The batch file will stop.)
```

Notes

The ECHO message is not the same as the REM message. REM is affected by an ECHO OFF command. The message on the line with the REM subcommand is not displayed if ECHO is off. The message on the line with ECHO is always displayed.

You can suppress the display of a single batch file line by using the @ as the first character in a line. By using the line

    @ECHO OFF

the command ECHO OFF is not displayed on-screen.

Once you suppress echo in a batch file, you must reissue ECHO.ON or exit a batch file to activate echo. If echo is turned off, and a second batch file is called, echo remains off.

To suppress the output of a command, use I/O redirection to the null device (NUL). For example, to suppress the file or files copied message when you are using COPY, type

COPY file1.ext file2.ext >NUL

The command's output is sent to the null device and is not displayed on-screen.

FOR..IN..DO

Batch Subcommand

Purpose

Permits repeated processing of an MS-DOS command.

Syntax

FOR %%variable IN (set) DO command

variable is a single letter.

set is one or more words or file specifications. The file specification is in the form *d:path\filename.ext.* You can use wildcards.

command is the MS-DOS command to be performed for each word or file in the set.

Rules

The following rules apply to the FOR..IN..DO command:

- You can use more than one word or a full file specification in the set. Separate words or file specifications by spaces or commas.

- %%variable becomes each literal word or full file specification in the set. If you use wildcard characters, FOR..IN..DO executes once for each file that matches the wildcard file specification.

- You can use path names.

- You cannot nest FOR..IN..DO subcommands (put two of these subcommands on the same line). You can use other batch subcommands with FOR..IN..DO.

- Wildcards (* or ?) in file names are valid in this command.

Example

This example uses FOR..IN..DO in a batch file called FORMAT.BAT that permits you to format only drive A: or drive B:.

```
ECHO OFF
IF %1. == . GOTO NONE
FOR %%a IN (a:, A:, b:, B:) DO IF %1 ==
    %%a GOTO FORMAT
ECHO You don't really mean to format %1,
    do you?
GOTO END
:NONE
ECHO You did not specify the drive (B), e.g.
    FORMAT B:
ECHO Please try the command again.
GOTO END
:FORMAT
XFORMAT   %1
:END
```

This batch file first tests for an empty parameter %1 because MS-DOS gives errors when testing anything against an empty string. The next command tests whether the designated disk drive is A or B, in both upper- and lowercase versions. If the letters match, processing jumps to where the file invokes the FORMAT command. If no match is found, processing drops to an error message and then jumps to END.

Note

set can contain literal words, separated by spaces. set replaces %%variable when the command executes. You can use FOR..IN..DO from the DOS command line with the following syntax:

FOR %%variable IN (set) DO command

GOTO

Batch Subcommand

Purpose

Transfers control to the line following the label in the batch file and continues batch file execution from that line.

Syntax

GOTO label

label is the name used for one or more characters, preceded by a colon. Only the first eight characters of the label name are significant.

Rules

The following rules apply to GOTO:

- The label must be the first item on a line in a batch file and must start with a colon (:).

- When GOTO label is executed, MS-DOS jumps to the line following the label and continues execution of the batch file.

- A label is never executed. MS-DOS uses the label only as the jump-to marker for the GOTO subcommand.

- If you issue a GOTO command with a nonexistent label, MS-DOS issues an error message and stops processing the batch file.

Example

This sample batch file uses GOTO and a label:

```
:START
DIR B:
PAUSE
GOTO START
```

As the first character in the line, the colon designates that the name START is a label. When this batch file is run, MS-DOS displays a list of the files on drive B and pauses. The final line directs MS-DOS to go to the :START line and execute the batch file again.

This batch file continues perpetually until you press **Ctrl-Break** or **Ctrl-C** to stop the action. (Unless it is absolutely necessary, do not use Ctrl-Break to stop a batch-file execution.)

IF

Batch Subcommand

Purpose

Permits conditional execution of an MS-DOS command.

Syntax

IF *NOT* **condition command**

NOT tests for the opposite of the **condition** (executes the command if the condition is false).

condition is what is being tested and can be one of the following:

ERRORLEVEL number   MS-DOS tests the exit code (0 to 255) of the program. If the exit code is greater than or equal to the number, the condition is true.

string1 == string2   MS-DOS tests whether these two alphanumeric strings are identical.

EXIST *d:path\filename.ext*   MS-DOS tests whether the file *d:path\filename.ext* is in the specified drive or path (if you specify a drive name or path name), or is on the current disk drive and directory.

command is any valid MS-DOS command or batch subcommand except another IF statement. You cannot put two or more IF subcommands on the same line.

Rules

The following rules apply for IF commands:

- The only MS-DOS programs that leave exit codes are BACKUP, DISKCOMP, DISKCOPY, FORMAT, GRAFTABL, KEYB, REPLACE, RESTORE, SETVER, and XCOPY. Using an **ERROR-LEVEL** condition with a program that does not leave an exit code is meaningless.

- For **string1 == string2**, MS-DOS makes a literal, character-by-character comparison of the two strings. The comparison is based on the ASCII character set, and upper- and lowercase letters are distinguished.

- When you are using **string1 == string2** with the parameter markers (%0 to %9), neither string may be null. If either string is null, MS-DOS displays a Syntax error message and aborts the batch file.

Examples

The batch file, MOVE.BAT, copies and deletes files, and uses IF to eliminate the potential disaster that may result from mistyping or omitting the directory name.

```
ECHO OFF
CLS
IF NOT EXIST C:\%1 GOTO ERROR1
COPY C:\%1 C:\%2 /V
IF NOT EXIST C:\%2\%1 GOTO ERROR2
ERASE C:\%1
GOTO EXIT
:ERROR1
ECHO The file (%1) does not exist...
GOTO EXIT
:ERROR2
ECHO The copy of C:\%1 to C:\%2 was
unsuccessful!
ECHO C:\%1 was not erased.
:EXIT
```

This batch file tests whether the new file exists and is
copied successfully. You combine C:\ with %1, the file
name, and %2, which is the subdirectory that will hold
the copied file. The result is a complete file name
(C:\%2\%1), which is used in the test for existence.
If the file exists, the COPY command was probably
successful. If, however, anything is wrong, the batch file
does not erase the original. This line is the "safety play."
It does nothing destructive in case something has failed.
When you create batch files, take the approach that
everything must be right before any files are destroyed.

This section presents a practical example that illustrates
the string-comparison option of IF. The example creates
a special batch file called FMAT.BAT to enable you to
format a 720K diskette in a 1.44M drive.

Suppose that drive A is your 1.44M drive, and
FORMAT.COM resides in the directory C:\DOS. Now
create the following batch file and call it FMAT.BAT:

```
@ECHO OFF
IF %1. == . GOTO F144
IF %1. == 720. GOTO F720
GOTO END
:F144
ECHO Formatting drive A as a 1.44M diskette.
C:\DOS\FORMAT A:
GOTO END
:F720
ECHO Formatting drive A as a 720K diskette.
C:\DOS\FORMAT A: /F:720
:END
```

In this command, the IF subcommand is used to test for
the equivalence of two strings. Remember that strings
are defined as sets of arbitrary (any) characters of
arbitrary (any) length. The assumption is that no
parameter is given (you type only FMAT), then the disk
in drive A will be formatted as the default 1.44M
diskette. However, if the parameter is 720 (you type
FMAT 720), the diskette in drive A will be formatted as
a 720K diskette.

The first test was for an empty parameter. If the parameter is nonexistent, then the GOTO F144 command is executed. If the first parameter is not empty, however, then a test is made to see if the parameter is equal to 720. If %1 does equal 720, then GOTO F720 is performed.

PAUSE

Batch Subcommand

Purpose

Suspends batch file processing until a key is pressed, and optionally displays a user's message.

Syntax

PAUSE *message*

message is a string of up to 121 characters.

Rules

The following rules apply to the PAUSE command:

- Regardless of ECHO's setting, MS-DOS displays
  `Strike a key when ready . . .`

- MS-DOS suspends the processing of the batch file until you press any key. Afterward, MS-DOS continues processing the batch file's lines. To end a batch file's processing, press **Ctrl-Break** or **Ctrl-C**.

Examples

Because the `Strike any key when ready . . .` message of PAUSE always shows on-screen, you can phrase your batch file message to take advantage of this line. For example, you can use these lines:

ECHO OFF
CLS
ECHO Place the proper disk into drive A,
ECHO and when the message appears,

ECHO press Enter to continue
ECHO or press Ctrl-Break
ECHO and then Y to stop the file.
PAUSE

This set of lines yields the following screen:

```
Place the proper disk into drive A,
and when the message appears,
press Enter to continue
or press Ctrl-Break
and then Y to stop the file.
Strike a key when ready . . .
```

You can rephrase your message as follows:

ECHO OFF
CLS
ECHO Place the proper disk into drive A.
ECHO If the disk is not available,
ECHO press Ctrl-Break and then Y
ECHO to stop the file, or
ECHO . . . .
ECHO [hard space]
PAUSE

This set of lines displays the following message:

```
Place the proper disk into drive A.
If the disk is not available,
press Ctrl-Break and then Y
to stop the file, or
. . . . . . . . . . . . . . . . . . . .
Strike a key when ready...
```

Adding the following two lines to this batch file before
the pause command makes it much cleaner on-screen:

ECHO . . . .
ECHO hard space

The first line draws a dotted line to separate the message
you create with ECHO commands in the batch file from
the message that the PAUSE command gives.

The second line is created by typing **ECHO**, pressing
the **space bar** to skip a space, and then holding down the
Alt key as you type **255** at the numeric keypad. You see

the cursor move one space to the right when this hard space is added. This is a legitimate ECHO command. Only a blank line appears because ASCII 255 is a space.

REM

Batch Subcommand

Purpose

Displays a message within the batch file.

Syntax

REM *message*

message is a string of up to 123 characters.

Example

This example shows the beginning of a sample batch file with REM commands:

REM To run this program, make sure
REM the disk containing BASICA is in
REM drive A and the disk labeled
       CONTRACTS
REM is in drive B.
REM . . . .
REM (If you need to exit at this time,
REM hold down the REM Ctrl key and
REM press the Break key. When the system
REM asks you whether you want to
REM "Terminate batch job (Y/N)?"
REM press Y. The batch file will stop.)

When this batch file runs, MS-DOS displays the word REM followed by each remark line on-screen. MS-DOS does not execute anything on the line.

Because REM does not display messages in a tidy order, consider using the batch subcommand ECHO.

Both ECHO and REM statements are useful in a batch file. With ECHO OFF, REM protects comments you want to remain in the batch file but do not want to appear on-screen, and ECHO displays messages on-screen. REM comments can serve as documentation when you or others want to change the file later, and ECHO messages can provide on-screen guidance.

With ECHO ON, ECHO statements appear twice and REM statements once.

SHIFT

Batch Subcommand

Purpose

Shifts one position to the left the parameters given on the command line when the batch file is invoked.

Syntax

SHIFT

Rules

The following rules apply to the SHIFT command:

- When you use SHIFT, MS-DOS moves the command line parameters one position to the left.

- MS-DOS discards the former first parameter (%0).

- When you write a batch file to execute a command that works in pairs, such as RENAME, include two SHIFT commands instead of one. Each SHIFT command is an executable MS-DOS command.

Example

SHIFT commonly is used when you are handling an undetermined number of similar parameters. For instance, you can take a file called MOVE.BAT (one that moves files to a predetermined subdirectory) and generalize it so that it can move any number of files.

```
ECHO OFF
CLS
:START
IF NOT EXIST C:\%1 GOTO ERROR1
COPY C:\%1 C:\SUBDIR1 /V
ERASE C:\%1
SHIFT
IF %1. == . GOTO EXIT
GOTO START
GOTO EXIT
:ERROR1
ECHO The file (%1) does not exist...
:EXIT
```

To move any number of files, you can enter the following command:

MOVE COMP.COM ABACUS.EXE
SLIDE.EXE LINK.EXE ABSCOND.COM

MOVE.BAT substitutes the first file (COMP.COM) for %1, processes the file, and shifts the parameters so that the second file (ABACUS.EXE) now becomes %1, and so on.

DOS EDIT

EDIT is a full-screen editor. Using EDIT is similar to using a word processor. With EDIT's menu system, you easily can edit, cut and paste text, search and replace text, print, and save a file.

Although you can create small files faster with COPY CON, you cannot edit a COPY CON file as you are creating it. If you plan to do involved programming or text entry, you will find EDIT to be a useful utility.

Use EDIT to create, edit, and save batch, text, and other ASCII files. You also use EDIT to create source files for C, assembly language, or any programming language. You also can create control codes and special graphic characters that you want to use in a file.

Note that EDIT is a separate program with its own
commands and menus. EDIT must be running before
you can use its commands and menus.

The following section explains how to start the EDIT
program. This section explains how to create a file, enter
text, and save the file.

Starting EDIT

Purpose

Enables you to edit text files, such as batch files, in a
full-screen mode.

Syntax

*dc:pathc***EDIT** *d:path\\filename.ext* /B /G /H
/NOHI

Switches

/B	Places EDIT in black and white screen colors.
/G	Quickly writes to a CGA monitor (may cause "snow" on some monitors).
/H	Displays text in the maximum lines that your screen supports (43 for EGA and 50 for VGA).
/NOHI	Uses reverse video rather than high-intensity characters (for LCD screens).

To start EDIT

1. Type **EDIT**. Because EDIT is an external program,
    you may need to precede the command with a drive
    name and path.

2. Optionally, type a space and the drive name, path,
    and name of the file you want to create or edit. Do
    not use wildcard characters (* or ?).

3. You can use any of EDIT's switches to alter the appearance of EDIT on the screen.

4. Press Enter.

5. Choose EDIT's menus at the top of the screen. Menus may be accessed by pressing Alt and the highlighted letter of the menu name, or by selecting the menu with the mouse.

6. You can use any of EDIT's menu commands to edit the file, or use the File menu to Open, Save, or Print a file.

7. Press PgUp, PgDn, Home, End, and the cursor-movement keys to move the cursor.

8. From the File menu, select Save and then select Exit to save the file and exit EDIT. If you are creating a new file, you are prompted for a file name. If you edit a file without saving, you are asked whether you want to save the file. Select Yes to save the file, No if you do not want to save changes, or Cancel to continue editing the file.

EDIT Commands

Menu Command   *Description*

File Menu

New	Clears the current file, if any, and enables you to save the old file and then create a new file.
Open...	Loads a file from disk into memory for editing.
Save	Saves the current file to disk by the same name as was retrieved or enables you to select a name if a new file.
Save as...	Saves the current file in memory by a different name.

Print...	Prints the current file in memory to the printer.
Exit	Exits EDIT and provides you with the option to save the file if it has not been saved.

Menu Command	*Description*

Edit Menu

Cut	Removes the highlighted text from the file, but keeps the last text you cut in temporary memory.
Copy	Copies the highlighted text into temporary memory without removing the highlighted text.
Paste	Places cut or copied text from the temporary memory into the current file.
Clear	Removes the highlighted text from the file.

Search Menu

Find...	Locates text in the file.
Repeat Last Find	Repeats the last search that you conducted.
Replace...	Locates text in the file and replaces it with other text.

Options Menu

Display...	Changes the colors of the screen.
Help Path	Specifies where the EDIT help file can be found.

MS-DOS MESSAGES

MS-DOS messages fall into two groups: *general* MS-DOS messages and MS-DOS *device error* messages. The larger group, general MS-DOS messages, is listed first, followed by the device error messages.

For your implementation and version of MS-DOS, the actual wording of error messages may differ from those shown here. If you see a message you cannot locate in this guide, refer to your computer's MS-DOS manual.

General MS-DOS Messages

The following messages may appear when you start MS-DOS or use your computer. Messages that usually appear when you start MS-DOS are marked (start-up). Most start-up errors mean that MS-DOS did not start and you must reboot the system. Most of the other error messages mean that MS-DOS terminated (aborted) the program and returned to the system prompt (A>). The messages are listed in alphabetical order for easy reference.

```
Bad command or filename
```

ERROR: The name you entered is not valid for invoking a command, program, or batch file. You most frequently see this message for the following reasons:

- You misspelled a name.

- You omitted a needed disk drive or path name.

- You gave the parameters without the command name, such as typing **myfile** instead of **ws myfile** (omitting the ws for WordStar).

Check the spelling on the command line. Make sure that the command, program, or batch file is in the location specified (disk drive and directory path). Then try the command again.

```
Bad or missing Command Interpreter
```

ERROR (start-up): MS-DOS cannot find the command interpreter, normally COMMAND.COM. MS-DOS does not start.

If you are starting MS-DOS, this message means COMMAND.COM is not on the boot disk or that a version of COMMAND.COM from a previous MS-DOS version is on the disk. If you have used the SHELL directive of CONFIG.SYS, the message means that it is improperly phrased or that COMMAND.COM is not where you specified. Place another diskette that contains the operating system in the floppy disk drive and then reset the system. After MS-DOS has started, copy COMMAND.COM to the original start-up disk so that you can boot from that disk.

If resetting the system does not solve the problem, use a copy of your MS-DOS boot diskette to restart the computer. Copy COMMAND.COM from this diskette to the offending disk.

Bad or missing filename

WARNING (start-up): MS-DOS was requested to load a device driver that could not be located, an error occurred when the device driver was loaded, or a break address for the device driver was out of bounds for the size of RAM memory being used in the computer. MS-DOS will continue its boot but will not use the device driver *filename*. In place of *filename* is the actual name of the file that could not be found.

If MS-DOS loads, check your CONFIG.SYS file for the line DEVICE=*filename*. Make sure the line is spelled correctly and the device driver is where you specified. If this line is correct, reboot the system. If the message appears again, copy the file from its original diskette to the boot diskette and try booting MS-DOS again. If the error persists, the device driver is bad. Contact the dealer or publisher who sold it to you.

Batch file missing

ERROR: MS-DOS could not find the batch file it was processing. The batch file may have been erased or renamed. MS-DOS aborts the processing of the batch file.

If you renamed the batch file, rename it again, using the original name. If required, edit the batch file to ensure the file name does not get changed again.

If the file was erased, re-create the batch file from its backup file if possible. Edit the file to ensure the batch file does not erase itself.

```
Cannot load COMMAND, system halted
```

ERROR: MS-DOS attempted to reload COMMAND.COM, but the area where MS-DOS keeps track of available and used memory was destroyed, or the command processor was not found in the directory specified by the COMSPEC= entry. The system halts.

This message indicates either that COMMAND.COM was erased from the disk and directory you used when starting MS-DOS, or that the COMSPEC= entry in the environment was changed. Restart MS-DOS. If it does not start, the copy of COMMAND.COM was erased. Restart MS-DOS from the original master diskettes and copy COMMAND.COM to your other disk.

```
Cannot start COMMAND, exiting
```

ERROR: MS-DOS was directed to load an additional copy of COMMAND.COM, but could not. Either your CONFIG.SYS FILES= command is set too low, or you do not have enough free memory for another copy of COMMAND.COM.

If your system has 256K or more and FILES is less than 10, edit the CONFIG.SYS file on your start-up diskette and use FILES = 15 or FILES = 20, then reboot.

If the problem occurs again, you do not have enough memory in your computer or you have too many resident or background programs competing for memory space. Restart MS-DOS and load only essential resident or background programs. If necessary, eliminate unneeded device drivers or RAM disk software. Another alternative is to increase the amount of RAM memory in your system.

```
Current drive is no longer valid
```

WARNING: You have set the system prompt to PROMPT $p. At the system level, MS-DOS attempted to read the current directory for the disk drive and found the drive no longer valid.

If the current disk drive is set for a floppy disk, this warning appears when you do not have a diskette in the disk drive. MS-DOS reports a `Drive not ready` error. Enter the **F** command to fail or the **I** command to ignore the error. Then insert a floppy diskette into the disk drive.

The invalid drive error can also occur if you have a current networked or SUBST disk drive that has been deleted or disconnected. Simply change the current disk to a valid disk drive.

Directory already exists

ERROR: Either you or a program attempted to create a directory, and a directory or a file by the same name already exists.

Do a DIR of the disk. Make sure no file or directory exists with the same name. If adding the directory to the root directory, remove or move (copy, then erase) any unneeded files or directives.

Disk boot failure

ERROR (start-up): An error occurred when MS-DOS tried to load itself into memory. The diskette contained IO.SYS and MSDOS.SYS, but one of the two files could not be loaded. MS-DOS did not boot.

Try starting MS-DOS from the diskette again. If the error recurs, try booting MS-DOS from a diskette you know is good, such as a copy of your MS-DOS master diskette. If this action fails, you have a hardware disk drive problem. Contact your local dealer. If you can boot from a master MS-DOS diskette, however, use SYS to transfer DOS to the diskette causing the error.

Divide overflow

ERROR: A program attempted to divide by zero. MS-DOS aborts the program. Either the program was incorrectly entered, or it contained a flaw in logic. With a well-written program, this error should never occur. If you wrote the program, correct the error and try the program again. If you purchased the program, report the problem to the dealer or publisher.

This message also can appear when you are attempting to format a RAM disk. Make sure you are formatting the correct disk and try again.

```
Error in EXE file
```

ERROR: MS-DOS detected an error while attempting to load a program stored in an .EXE file. The problem is in the relocation information MS-DOS needs to load the program. This problem can occur if the .EXE file has been altered in any way.

Restart MS-DOS and try the program again, this time using a backup copy of the program. If the message reappears, the program is flawed. Try copying the EXE file from an original disk. If the problem still exists, contact the manufacturer of the program.

```
Error loading operating system
```

ERROR (start-up): A disk error occurred while MS-DOS was loading itself from the hard disk. MS-DOS does not boot.

Restart the computer. If the error occurs after several tries, restart MS-DOS from the floppy disk drive. If the hard disk does not respond (that is, you cannot run DIR or CHKDSK without getting an error), you have a problem with the hard disk. Contact your local dealer. If the hard disk does respond, use the SYS command to put another copy of MS-DOS onto your hard disk. You may need to copy COMMAND.COM to the hard disk also.

```
EXEC failure
```

ERROR: MS-DOS encountered an error while reading a command or program from the disk, or the CONFIG.SYS FILES= command has too low a value.

Increase the number of FILES in the CONFIG.SYS file of your start-up disk to 15 or 20, then restart MS-DOS. If the error recurs, you may have a problem with the disk. Use a backup copy of the program and try again. If

the backup copy works, copy it over the offending copy
of your start-up disk.

If an error occurs in the copying process, you have a
flawed diskette or hard disk. If the problem is with a
diskette, copy the files from the flawed diskette to
another diskette and reformat or retire the original
diskette. If the problem is with the hard disk,
immediately back up your files and run RECOVER on
the offending file. If the problem persists, your hard disk
may have a hardware failure.

```
File allocation table bad, drive d Abort,
Retry, Fail?
```

WARNING: MS-DOS encountered a problem in the
File Allocation Table (FAT) of the disk in drive D.
Type **R** for Retry several times. If this does not solve the
problem, use **A** for Abort.

If you are using a diskette, attempt to copy all the files to
another diskette and then reformat or retire the original
diskette. If you are using a hard disk, back up all files on
the disk and reformat the hard disk. The disk is unusable
until reformatted.

```
File creation error
```

ERROR: Either a program or MS-DOS attempted to add
a new file to the directory or to replace an existing file,
but failed.

If the file already exists, use the ATTRIB command to
check whether the file is marked as read-only. If the
read-only flag is set and you want to change or erase the
file, use ATTRIB to remove the read-only flag and then
try again.

If the problem is not a read-only flag, run CHKDSK
without the /F switch to determine whether the directory
is full, the disk is full, or some other problem exists with
the disk.

```
File not found
```

ERROR: MS-DOS could not find the file you specified.
The file is not on the correct diskette or in the correct
directory; or you misspelled the disk drive name, path

name, or file name. Check these possibilities and try the command again.

```
Filename device driver cannot be initialized
```

WARNING (start-up): In CONFIG.SYS, either the parameters in the device driver *filename* are incorrect, or the DEVICE line is in error. Check for incorrect parameters and for phrasing errors in the DEVICE line. Edit the DEVICE line in the CONFIG.SYS file, save the file, and restart MS-DOS.

```
Incorrect MS-DOS version
```

ERROR: The copy of the file holding the command you just entered is from a different version of MS-DOS.

Get a copy of the command from the appropriate version of MS-DOS (usually from your copy of the MS-DOS master diskette) and try the command again. If the disk or diskette you are using has been updated to hold new versions of the MS-DOS programs, copy those versions over the old ones.

If a utility gives you this error, then you may "trick" the utility into believing an older version of DOS is running. Use the SETVER command to enter a DOS version the utility should recognize.

```
Insert disk with \COMMAND.COM in drive d

Press any key to continue
```

INFORMATIONAL and WARNING: MS-DOS needed to reload COMMAND.COM but could not find it on the start-up disk.

If you are using diskettes, probably the diskette in drive A has been changed. Place a diskette containing a good copy of COMMAND.COM in drive A and press a key.

```
Insert disk with batch file

Press any key to continue
```

INFORMATIONAL: MS-DOS is attempting to execute the next command from a batch file, but the diskette containing the batch file was removed from the disk drive.

Put the diskette containing the batch file into the disk
drive and press a key to continue.

```
Insert diskette for drive d and
strike any key when ready
```

INFORMATIONAL: On a system with one floppy disk
drive, either you or a program specified the tandem disk
drive D (A or B). This drive is different from the current
disk drive.

If the correct diskette is in the disk drive, press a key.
Otherwise, put the correct diskette into the floppy disk
drive and then press a key.

```
Insufficient disk space
```

WARNING or ERROR: The disk does not have enough
free space to hold the file being written. All MS-DOS
programs terminate when this problem occurs, but some
non-DOS programs continue.

If you think the disk has enough room to hold this file,
run CHKDSK to see whether there is a problem with the
disk or diskette. Sometimes when you terminate
programs early by pressing Ctrl-Break, MS-DOS is
unable to do the necessary clean-up work. When this
happens, disk space is temporarily trapped. CHKDSK
can "free" these areas.

If you simply have run out of disk space, free some disk
space or use a different diskette or hard disk. Try the
command again.

```
Insufficient memory
```

ERROR: The computer does not have enough free RAM
memory to execute the program or command.

If you loaded a resident program such as PRINT,
GRAPHICS, MODE, or MIRROR, restart MS-DOS and
try the command before loading any resident program. If
this method fails, remove any unneeded device driver or
RAM-disk software from the CONFIG.SYS file and
restart MS-DOS again. If this action fails, your computer
does not have enough memory to run this command.
You must increase your RAM memory.

Intermediate file error during pipe

ERROR: MS-DOS is unable to create or write to one or both of the intermediate files it uses when piping (|) information between programs. The disk or root directory is full, or MS-DOS cannot locate the files. The most frequent cause is a lack of disk space.

Run the DIR command on the root directory of the current disk drive. Make sure you have enough free space and enough room in the root directory for two additional files. If you do not have enough room, make room on the disk by deleting, or copying and deleting, files. You may also copy the necessary files to a different diskette with sufficient room.

A program may be deleting files, including the temporary files MS-DOS uses. If this is the case, you should correct the program, contact the dealer or program publisher, or avoid using the program with piping.

Internal stack overflow System halted

ERROR: Your programs and MS-DOS have exhausted the stack, the memory space that is reserved for temporary use. This problem is usually caused by a rapid succession of hardware devices demanding attention (interrupts). If you want to prevent this error from ever occurring, add the STACKS directive to your CONFIG.SYS file. If the directive is already in your CONFIG.SYS file, then increase the number of stacks specified.

Invalid COMMAND.COM in drive d

WARNING: MS-DOS tried to reload from the disk in drive D and found the file was of a different version of MS-DOS. You will see a message instructing you to insert a diskette with the correct version and press a key. Follow the directions given by the message.

If you frequently use the diskette that was originally in the disk drive, copy the correct version of COMMAND.COM to that diskette.

Invalid COMMAND.COM, system halted

ERROR: MS-DOS could not find COMMAND.COM on the hard disk. MS-DOS halts and must be restarted.

COMMAND.COM may have been erased, or the COMSPEC= setting in the environment may have been changed. Restart the computer from the hard disk. If you see a message that indicates COMMAND.COM is missing, that file was erased. Restart MS-DOS from a diskette and recopy COMMAND.COM to the root directory of the hard disk or to wherever your SHELL command directs, if you have used this command in your CONFIG.SYS file.

If you restart MS-DOS and this message appears later, a program or batch file is erasing COMMAND.COM or is altering the COMSPEC= parameter. If a batch file is erasing COMMAND.COM, edit the batch file. If a program is erasing COMMAND.COM, contact the dealer or publisher that sold you the program. If COMSPEC= is being altered, either edit the offending batch file or program, or place COMMAND.COM in the subdirectory expected by your program or batch file.

Invalid directory

ERROR: One of the following errors occurred:

- You specified a directory name that does not exist.

- You misspelled the directory name.

- The directory path is on a different disk.

- You forgot to give the path character (\) at the beginning of the name.

- You did not separate the directory names with the path character. Check your directory names, ensure that the directories do exist, and try the command again.

Invalid disk change

WARNING: The diskette in the 720K, 1.2M, or 1.44M disk drive was changed while a program had open files to be written to the diskette. You will see the message Abort, Retry, Fail. Place the correct diskette in the disk drive and type **R** for Retry.

```
Invalid drive in search path
```

WARNING: One specification you gave to the PATH command has an invalid disk drive name, or a named disk drive is nonexistent or hidden temporarily by a SUBST or JOIN command.

Use PATH to check the paths you instructed MS-DOS to search. If you gave a nonexistent disk drive name, use the PATH command again and enter the correct search paths. If the problem is temporary because of a SUBST or JOIN command, you can again use PATH to enter the paths, but leave out or correct the wrong entry. Or you can just ignore the warning message.

```
Invalid drive specification
```

ERROR: This message occurs for the following reasons:

- You entered the name of an invalid or nonexistent disk drive as a parameter to a command.

- You specified the same disk drive for the source and destination, which is not permitted for the command.

- By not specifying a parameter, you have defaulted to the same source and destination disk drive.

Remember that certain MS-DOS commands (such as SUBST and JOIN) temporarily hide disk drive names while the command is in effect. Check the disk drive names. If the command is objecting to a missing parameter and defaulting to the wrong disk drive, explicitly name the correct disk drive.

```
Invalid drive specification
Specified drive does not exist
or is non-removable
```

ERROR: One of the following errors occurred:

- You specified the name of a nonexistent disk drive.

- You named the hard disk drive when using commands for diskettes only.

- You did not specify a disk drive name and defaulted to the hard disk when using commands for diskettes only.

- You named or defaulted to a RAM-disk drive when using commands for a "real" floppy diskette only.

Remember that certain MS-DOS commands (such as SUBST and JOIN) temporarily hide disk drive names while the command is in effect. Check the disk drive name you gave and try the command again.

Invalid environment size specified

WARNING: You have given the SHELL directive in CONFIG.SYS. The environment-size switch (/E:size) contains either non-numeric characters or a number that is less than 160 or greater than 32768.

If you are using the SHELL /E:size switch of MS-DOS V3.1, *size* is the number of 16-byte memory blocks, not the number of bytes.

Check the form of your CONFIG.SYS SHELL directive; the form needs to be exact. There must be a colon between /E and *size*; there must not be a comma or space between or within the /E: and the *size* characters; and the number in *size* should be greater than or equal to 160, but less than or equal to 32768.

Invalid partition table

ERROR (start-up): While you were attempting to start MS-DOS from the hard disk, MS-DOS detected a problem in the hard disk's partition information.

Restart MS-DOS from a diskette. Back up all files from the hard disk if possible. Run FDISK to correct the problem. If you change the partition information, you must reformat the hard disk and restore all its files.

Invalid path

ERROR: One of the following errors has occurred to a path name you entered:

- The path name contains illegal characters.

- The name has more than 63 characters.

- One of the directory names within the path is misspelled or does not exist.

Check the spelling of the path name. If needed, do a DIR of the disk and ensure that the directory you have specified does exist and that you have the correct path name. Be sure that the path name contains 63 characters or less. If necessary, change the current directory to a directory "closer" to the file and shorten the path name.

```
Invalid STACK parameter
```

WARNING (start-up): One of the following errors has occurred to the STACKS directive in your CONFIG.SYS file: a comma is missing between the number of stacks and the size of the stack; the number of stack frames is not in the range of 8 to 64; the stack size is not in the range of 32 to 512; you have omitted either the number of stack frames or the stack size; or either the stack frame or the stack size (but not both) is 0. MS-DOS continues to start but ignores the STACKS directive.

Check the STACKS directive in your CONFIG.SYS file. Edit and save the file, and restart MS-DOS.

```
Invalid switch character
```

WARNING: You have used VDISK.SYS in your CONFIG.SYS file. VDISK encountered a switch (/) but the character immediately following it was not an *E* for *extended memory*. MS-DOS loads VDISK and attempts to install VDISK in low (nonextended) memory. Either you have misspelled the */E* switch, or you have left a space between the / and the *E*. Edit and save your CONFIG.SYS file, and restart MS-DOS.

```
Memory allocation error
Cannot load COMMAND, system halted
```

ERROR: A program destroyed the area where MS-DOS keeps track of in-use and available memory. You must restart MS-DOS.

If this error occurs again with the same program, the program has a flaw. Use a backup copy of the program. If the problem persists, contact the dealer or program manufacturer.

```
Missing operating system
```

ERROR (start-up): The MS-DOS hard disk partition
entry is marked as "bootable" (able to start MS-DOS),
but the MS-DOS partition does not have a copy of
MS-DOS on it. MS-DOS does not boot.

Start MS-DOS from a diskette. If you have existing files
on the hard disk, back up the files. Issue FORMAT /S to
put a copy of the operating system on the hard disk. If
necessary, restore the files that you backed up.

```
No free file handles
Cannot start COMMAND, exiting
```

ERROR: MS-DOS could not load an additional copy of
COMMAND.COM because no file handles (FILES=)
were available.

Edit the CONFIG.SYS file on your start-up disk to
increase the number of file handles (using the FILES
command) by five. Restart MS-DOS and try the
command again.

```
Non-System disk or disk error
Replace and press any key when ready
```

ERROR (start-up): Your diskette or hard disk does not
contain MS-DOS, or a read error occurred when you
started the system. MS-DOS does not boot.

If you are using a floppy disk system, put a bootable
diskette in drive A and press a key.

The most frequent cause of this message on hard disk
systems is leaving a nonbootable diskette in disk drive A
with the door closed. Open the door to disk drive A and
press a key. MS-DOS will boot from the hard disk.

```
Not enough memory
```

ERROR: The computer does not have enough free RAM
memory to execute the program or command. If you
loaded a resident program such as PRINT, GRAPHICS,
SideKick, or ProKey, restart MS-DOS and try the
command again before loading any resident program. If
this method fails, remove any unneeded device driver or
RAM-disk software from the CONFIG.SYS file and
restart MS-DOS again. If this option fails also, your

computer does not have enough memory to run this command. You must increase your RAM memory.

```
Out of environment space
```

WARNING: MS-DOS is unable to add to the environment any more strings from the SET command. The environment cannot be expanded. This error occurs when you load a resident program, such as MODE, PRINT, GRAPHICS, or MIRROR.

Refer to the SHELL command for information about expanding the default space for the environment using the /E switch with COMMAND.COM.

```
Parameter format not correct - parm
```

ERROR: You entered a parameter using an incorrect form. You may have forgotten to place a slash (/) in front of a switch or a colon for the drive designation.

```
Path not found
```

ERROR: A file or directory path you named does not exist. You may have misspelled the file name or directory name, or you omitted a path character (\) between directory names or between the final directory name and file name. Another possibility is that the file or directory does not exist where you specified. Check these possibilities and try again.

```
Path too long
```

ERROR: You specified a path name that exceeds the 63-character limit of MS-DOS. Either the name is too long, or you omitted a space between file names. Check the command line. If the phrasing is correct, you must change to a directory that is closer to the file you want and try the command again.

```
Program too big to fit in memory
```

ERROR: The computer does not have enough memory to load the program or command you invoked.

If you have any resident programs loaded (such as PRINT, GRAPHICS, or SideKick), restart MS-DOS and try the command again without loading the resident programs. If this message appears again, reduce the number of buffers (BUFFERS=) in the CONFIG.SYS file, eliminate unneeded device drivers or RAM-disk software, and restart MS-DOS again. If these actions do not solve the problem, your computer does not have enough RAM memory for the program or command. You must increase the amount of RAM memory in your computer to run this command.

Required parameter missing

ERROR: You did not specify a necessary parameter. Check the syntax to see how many parameters are required. For example, if you specify FORMAT without specifying the drive to format, you will encounter this error message.

Sharing violation

WARNING: With the file-sharing program (SHARE.EXE) loaded, you or one of your programs attempted to access a file by using a sharing mode not allowed at this time. Another program or computer has temporary control over the file.

You will see the message Abort, Retry, Ignore. Press R for Retry several times. If the problem persists, press A for Abort. If you abort, however, any data currently being manipulated by the program will be lost.

Syntax error

ERROR: You phrased a command improperly by omitting needed information; giving extraneous information; putting an extra space in a file name or path name; or using an incorrect switch. Check the command line for these possibilities and try the command again.

Too many block devices

WARNING (start-up): There are too many DEVICE directives in your CONFIG.SYS file. MS-DOS continues to start but does not install any additional device drivers.

MS-DOS can handle only 26 block devices. The block devices created by the DEVICE directives plus the number of block devices MS-DOS automatically created exceed 26. Remove any unnecessary DEVICE directives in your CONFIG.SYS file and restart MS-DOS.

```
Too many parameters - parms
```

ERROR: You have given too many parameters in a command. Check to see if you put an extra space in the command or forgot to place a slash (/) in front of a switch.

```
Top level process aborted, cannot continue
```

ERROR (start-up): COMMAND.COM or another MS-DOS command detected a disk error, and you chose the A (abort) option. MS-DOS cannot finish starting itself, and the system halts.

Try to start MS-DOS again. If the error recurs, use a floppy diskette (if starting from the hard disk) or a different floppy diskette (if starting from floppy diskettes) to start MS-DOS. After it has started, use the SYS command to put another copy of the operating system on the disk, and copy COMMAND.COM to the disk. If MS-DOS reports an error during the copying, the disk or diskette is bad. Either reformat or retire the floppy diskette, or back up and reformat the hard disk.

```
Unable to create directory
```

ERROR: Either you or a program attempted to create a directory, and one of the following has occurred:

- A directory by the same name already exists.

- A file by the same name already exists.

- You are adding a directory to the root directory, and the root directory is full.

- The directory name has illegal characters or is a device name.

Do a DIR of the disk. Make sure that no file or directory already exists with the same name. If adding the directory to the root directory, remove or move (copy, then erase) any unneeded files or directives. Check the spelling of the directory and ensure that the command is properly phrased.

```
Unrecognized command in CONFIG.SYS
```

WARNING (start-up): MS-DOS detected an improperly phrased directive in CONFIG.SYS. The directive is ignored, and MS-DOS continues to start; but MS-DOS does not indicate the incorrect line. Examine the CONFIG.SYS file, looking for improperly phrased or incorrect directives. Edit the line, save the file, and restart MS-DOS.

MS-DOS Device Error Messages

When MS-DOS detects an error while reading or writing to disk drives or other devices, one of the following messages appears:

> *type* error reading *device*

> *type* error writing *device*

Type is the type of error, and *device* is the device at fault. If the device is a floppy disk drive, do not remove the diskette from the drive. Refer to this section which lists the types of error messages that may appear, and describes possible causes and corrective actions.

```
Bad call format
```

A device driver was given a requested header with an incorrect length. The problem is with the applications software making the call.

```
Bad command
```

The device driver issued an invalid or unsupported command to the device. The problem may be with the device driver software or with other software trying to use the device driver.

```
Bad format call
```

The device driver at fault passed an incorrect header length to MS-DOS. If you wrote this device driver, you must rewrite it to correct the problem. For a purchased program, contact the dealer or publisher who sold you the driver.

```
Bad unit
```

An invalid subunit number was passed to the device driver. The problem may be with the device driver software or with other software trying to use the device driver. Contact the dealer who sold you the device driver.

```
Drive not ready
```

An error occurred while MS-DOS tried to read or write to the disk drive. For floppy disk drives, the drive door may be open, the micro diskette may not be inserted, or the diskette may not be formatted. For hard disk drives, the drive may not be properly prepared or you may have a hardware problem.

```
General failure
```

This is a "catch all" error message not covered elsewhere. The error usually occurs when you use an unformatted diskette or hard disk, or when you leave the disk drive door open.

```
Lock violation
```

With the file-sharing program (SHARE.EXE) or network software loaded, one of your programs attempted to access a locked file. Your best choice is Retry. Then try Abort. If you choose A, however, any data in memory will be lost.

```
No paper
```

The printer is either out of paper or not turned on.

```
Non-DOS disk
```

The FAT has invalid information. This diskette is unusable. You can Abort and run CHKDSK on the diskette to see whether any corrective action is possible. If CHKDSK fails, your other alternative is to reformat

the diskette. Reformatting, however, will destroy any
remaining information on the diskette. If you use more
than one operating system, the diskette has probably
been formatted under the operating system you are using
and should not be reformatted.

Not ready

The device is not ready and cannot receive or transmit
data. Check the connections, make sure that the power is
on, and check to see whether the device is ready.

Read fault

MS-DOS is unable to read the data, usually from a hard
disk or diskette. Check the disk drive doors and make
sure the diskette is properly inserted.

Sector not found

The disk drive is unable to locate the sector on the
diskette or hard disk platter. This error is usually the
result of a defective spot on the disk or of defective
drive electronics. Some copy-protection schemes also
use this method (a defective spot) to prevent
unauthorized duplication of the diskette.

Seek

The disk drive could not locate the proper track on the
diskette or hard disk platter. This error is usually the
result of a defective spot on the diskette or hard disk
platter, an unformatted disk, or drive electronics
problems.

Sharing violation

With the file-sharing program (SHARE.EXE) or
network software loaded, your programs attempted to
access a file by using a sharing mode not specified for
that file. Your best response is Retry; if that doesn't
work, try Abort.

Write fault

MS-DOS could not write the data to this device. Perhaps
you inserted the diskette improperly, or you left the disk
drive door open. Another possibility is an electronics

failure in the floppy or hard disk drive. The most frequent cause is a bad spot on the diskette.

```
Write protect
```

The diskette is write-protected.

MS-DOS will display one of these error messages followed by the line:

```
Abort, Retry, Ignore?
```

If you press **A** for Abort, MS-DOS will end the program that requested the read or write condition. Typing **R** for Retry will cause MS-DOS to try the operation again. If you press **I** for Ignore, MS-DOS will skip the operation, and the program will continue. However, some data may be lost when Ignore is used.

The order of preference, unless stated differently under the message, is **R**, **A**, and **I**. You should retry the operation at least twice. If the condition persists, you must decide whether to abort the program or ignore the error. If you ignore the error, data may be lost. If you abort, data still being processed by the program and not yet written to the disk will be lost. Remember that **I** is the least desirable option and that **A** should be used after Retry has failed at least two times.

DOS SURVIVAL GUIDE

Note: An asterisk (*) designates a CONFIG.SYS directive.

To	Use
Analyze a disk	CHKDSK
Automatically find files	APPEND, PATH
Automatically run a file at startup	AUTOEXEC.BAT
Print from the background	PRINT

Back up files	BACKUP, COPY, XCOPY
Back up disks	BACKUP, DISKCOPY
Change a code page	CHCP, KEYB, MODE
Change the active display	MODE
Change the baud rate	MODE
Change the key repeat rate	MODE
Change the console	CTTY
Change the current directory	CHDIR (CD)
Change the current disk drive	d:
Change disk buffers	BUFFERS*
Change the disk label	LABEL
Change the environment	SET
Change file attributes	ATTRIB
Change a file name	RENAME (REN)
Change/set location of the command interpreter	SHELL*
Change program input	<
Change program output	>,>>
Clear the video display	CLS
Combine disks	JOIN
Combine files	COPY
Compare diskettes	DISKCOMP
Compare files	COMP, FC
Concatenate files	COPY
Connect disk drives	JOIN
Control Ctrl-Break	BREAK, BREAK*
Control verification of files	VERIFY
Copy diskettes	DISKCOPY, COPY, XCOPY

Copy backup files	RESTORE
Copy files	COPY, REPLACE, XCOPY
Create a macro	DOSKEY
Create a subdirectory	MKDIR (MD)
Display available RAM	CHKDSK, MEM
Display the current code page	CHCP, MODE
Display the date	DATE
Display the version of DOS	VER
Display environmental variables	SET
Display contents of a file	MORE, TYPE
Display a list of directories	CHKDSK /V, TREE, DIR /S
Display a list of files	DIR, CHKDSK /V, TREE /F
Display national-language characters	CHCP, GRAFTABL, KEYB, MODE
Display the time	TIME
Display the volume label	VOL, LABEL, DIR, CHKDSK
Erase a character	Backspace
Erase a directory	RMDIR (RD)
Erase a disk label	LABEL
Erase files	DEL, ERASE
Execute several DOS commands with one command	Batch file
Find disk free space	CHKDSK, DIR
Find a file	CHKDSK /V, TREE /F, DIR /S

Find a word or phrase in a file	FIND
Freeze the video display	Ctrl-NumLock, Pause
Ignore a line	Esc
Load file-sharing software	SHARE
Pause the display	Ctrl-Num Lock, Pause, Ctrl-S
Pipe output between programs	|
Place DOS on a disk	SYS, FORMAT /S
Prepare a disk	FORMAT, FDISK
Print graphics	GRAPHICS
Print the display	Shift-PrintSc, GRAPHICS
Print on the display and the printer	Ctrl-PrintSc
Print a file	PRINT, Typefile>PRN, COPY
Protect a disk from tragedies	MIRROR
Reassign disk drives	ASSIGN, JOIN, SUBST
Reassign printers	MODE
Restore backup files	RESTORE
Restore an erased file	UNDELETE
Restore a formatted disk	UNFORMAT
Repair a file	RECOVER
Repair a disk	RECOVER, CHKDSK
Remove a directory	RMDIR (RD)
Remove files	DEL, ERASE
Run a program	program_name
Set alternative directories for programs	PATH

Set alternative directories for data files	APPEND
Set the country code	COUNTRY*
Set/change a code page	MODE, KEYB
Set/change checks on file writing	VERIFY
Set/change communications ports	MODE
Set/change displays	MODE
Set/change an environmental variable	SET
Set/change printers	MODE
Set/change internal stacks	STACKS*
Set/change the system date	DATE
Set/change the system prompt	PROMPT
Set/change the system time	TIME
Sort a file	SORT
Speed DOS	BUFFERS*, FASTOPEN
Start a device driver in reserved memory	DEVICEHIGH*
Start a program in reserved memory	LOADHIGH
Stop a running program	Ctrl-Break, Ctrl-C
Stop a running program and reset the computer	Ctrl-Alt-Del
Track deleted files	MIRROR
Trick a program into thinking an older version of DOS is being used	SETVER
Unfreeze the video display	Any key
Update files	REPLACE

Use a different disk drive	d:, ASSIGN, SUBST
Use a new device	DEVICE*
Use a subdirectory in place of a disk	SUBST

Index